The
Roo Club

Oliver Eade

www.olivereadebooks.org

Front cover artwork copyright © Fiona Ruiz

Cover image of a Queensland kangaroo © Oliver Eade

ISBN: 978-1-80440-195-8

Silver Quill Publishing

www.silverquillpublishing.com

Dedicated to Lucia, Beatriz, Olivia & Lara

'

'Forgiveness is the fragrance that the violet sheds on the heel that has crushed it.'

Saint Teresa of Calcutta

Acknowledgements

I am beholden to my dear wife, Yvonne, for proofreading *'The Roo Club'*, and for putting up with my ups and downs over the years. Also to Iona McGregor for her support and encouragement, as well as other writers in Silver Quill Publishing. I wish to thank my daughter, Fiona, for her cover design input.

Oliver Eade, May 2024

Reviews of some of the author's other publications:

Moon Rabbit
'...Moon Rabbit will lead children's imaginations to fantastical realms. It is a magical mix enhanced by gentle and ethereal illustrations...

Mairi Hedderwick, author of the Katie Morag books.

'...Enchanting tale of two children who embark on a dangerous mission... Ideal introduction into Chinese culture... to be enjoyed by children of all ages...'

A Good Read, Sunday Express, 2009

'Magical Experience...'

PA News, 2010

Northwards
'...A witty and heart-warming novel packed with adventure...'

Sunday Express, 2010

A Single Petal
'...Carefully researched, well plotted... full-blooded... .solidly grounded in traditional narrative rules...'

Alastair Mabbott, The Herald, 2013

'...There's an abundance of beauty in this book...: it is a sensitive, poetic account of the faith, fears and irresistible forces within a community...'

Raymond Hume, The Writer, 2020

The Terminus
'...Once you pick up this chilling book, be prepared to climb onto an emotional roller-coaster...'

Wendy Leighton-Porter, award winning author of the 'Shadows of the Past series', 2013

Parth Path
'...A momentous novel. The reader is drawn into a post-apocalyptic nightmare... In the face of overwhelming evil, good prevails...'

Iona Carroll, author of the 'Oisin Kelly series', 2018

The Kelpie's Eyes

'...An extraordinarily good fantasy novel... so well-handled that it grips throughout...'

Frost Magazine, 2018

In the Blink of an Eye

'...Powerful stories following key developments in medicine... clearly written and hugely informative...'

Ray Cartwright, Emeritus Professor of Medicine, University of Leeds

Chapter One

As she approaches, quietly, on tip toes, the sudden scatter of squabbling ducks, busily preening themselves whilst basking beside a Parliament Hill Fields pond, reminds Emily of the transience of happiness. When the birds noisily flap and splash down into the water in the middle of the pond, well away from her, their hysterical quacks muddle the girl's dark thoughts. Thoughts about death being her only release from interminable pain; thoughts that, but for the whispered words of her big brother, Jimmy, would be put into action in the same pond with pockets filled with stones...

...As once happened with that writer Jimmy told her about: Virginia Woolf.

She turns, leaving the ducks to quack amongst themselves about her rude intrusion into their wet little lives, and heads for her granny's house in the Vale of Health at the other end of Hampstead Heath.

Jimmy's suggestion. His alternative to death by drowning.

*****

"Hi, there. You the new girl? I'm Emily. My dad's a doctor. A surgeon. Cuts people open and all that... ugh!"

The other girl smiled. Briefly.

"Belinda," she responded. "Nice to meet you, Emily. And the only thing *my* dad cuts is a purple pimple on his chin when he shaves."

Emily giggled.

"It's gross!" said Belinda.

"Come and meet my friends over there," suggested Emily. "We're *all* into music, you know. Because of this school. I'm a pianist. Like my granny. She's famous. Played in the Carnegie Hall. Once. Bit old now. Hands too knobbly to play in concerts. She has loads of money, though. Lives by the Heath. Maybe–?"

"Introduce me to your friends, Emily," interrupted the other girl.

"Oh... right. Cool!"

Five girls, grouped together, looked up as Emily approached with the new girl.

"Hi guys! This is Belinda. New here. Comes from... erm...?"

Emily looked at Belinda.

"Fucking state school on the Northern Line. Left behind an annoying little sister for them to do something with so I can get on with my life. Here. Best girls' school in North London, Dad says."

"He's got a purple pimple on his chin," added Emily, grinning.

But Belinda ignored her. Instead, she turned her back on the girl who had so cheerfully befriended her, immediately entering into lively discussion with Emily's friends about the attributes of their school, how she'd love to get to know them all, share time with them, chill out.

So began Emily's nightmare...

*****

"Emily? What *are* you doing here? Shouldn't you be at...?" Granny halts mid-sentence on seeing a solitary tear emerge from the corner of one of her granddaughter's sorrowful eyes before snail-trailing down the girl's pale, young cheek. She opens her arms wide, hugs Emily and strokes her hair when the girl starts to sob uncontrollably. She takes her granddaughter into the sitting room where, for what seems an eternity, they sit together in silence, on the settee, the elderly pianist's arthritic arm resting across the girl's shoulders.

"Trouble at school?" Old Mabel finally asks.

Without looking up, her head now pressed against her granny's shrivelled bosom, Emily nods.

"Work? Exams?"

The granddaughter shakes her head.

"Boys?"

Emily giggles through her tears and shakes her head again.

"Mummy and Daddy okay? Getting on all right?"

Emily nods.

"The North London Festival of Music and Drama? You're worried that you, Lingling and Schubert won't get first place? Hellish difficult, the F minor Fantasy. Musically, not technically."

Emily looks up.

"I've lost my friends."

"Oh dear, that is careless. Where do you think you left them?"

"Granny!" Emily sits back. She wipes her tears with

the back of her hand and frowns at her grandmother. "That new girl I mentioned the other day..."

"Belinda?"

"Uh-huh!

"She's stolen my friends. I mean, not exactly stolen them. More like put them all against me. By doing things. Saying things. Even Lingling's being mean now. Can't see how we can go ahead with the Festival Competition. And whenever I practice the piano, I just see *her*. Belinda. With that look on her face. Puts me off. *And* she knows she's much better looking than me."

"Oh, no way! That is not possible."

"I daren't tell Mum. She'll only phone the school and make things a thousand times worse. As for Dad, he'd..."

"He'd go storming off to your school armed with a scalpel, right?"

Emily grins.

"Jimmy told me to come here."

"Big brother Jimmy who doesn't exist, right?"

"He *does*! Just that no one else can see or talk to him."

"Well, he did the right thing."

"I really came to the Heath to end it all in one of the ponds, but..."

"But Jimmy saw sense, right? Look, help yourself to whatever you can find in the kitchen. Muffins came out pretty well this morning. Jenny told me to make them. Must've been having words with your Jimmy."

Emily stares at her grandmother.

"Who's Jenny?" she asks.

"Get those muffins and a glass of milk, and I'll introduce you."

*****

Emily's phone rang. She had stopped messaging and social networking after Belinda peppered Snapchat, Instagram and Twitter with snide comments about her being 'weird'.

It was Lingling.

Ever hopeful, Emily eagerly answered.

Silence.

"Lingling?"

More silence.

"Is that you? You okay for a practice tomorrow?"

Giggles, then the phone went dead.

*****

"When I was a girl..."

Old Mabel pauses to take a bite out of a muffin. Emily grins.

"Like a hundred years ago?" the girl offers.

"Enough of your cheek, young lady. When I was a child, I had a best friend forever. I called her Jenny."

"And no else could see or hear her?"

"Or knew about her. See, I never went to a special school like you. Your great grandparents weren't wealthy."

"Yeah. Your dad worked on the railway. LNER, you said. All the way to Newcastle."

"Ticket conductor."

"And you got teased at school. Because—"

"We never talked about that. The 'other family', Jenny called them. In Newcastle."

"Weren't you curious? To know what they looked like."

"Not when all that teasing just about destroyed me. But Jenny helped me through it all. Jenny and Beethoven."

"Do you still talk to her?"

"Now why would a young girl like Jenny want to chill out with an old lady like me?"

"Because..." Emily pauses. She looks at the muffins, picks one up and holds it in front of her grandmother. "Because you're the best!"

"But there is someone she'd love to meet. I know it."

"Me?"

"You'd not see her. Or be able to talk with her."

"Hmm!"

"But your big brother, now?"

Emily's eyes light up.

"Jenny and Jimmy get together, like?"

"Who knows where that might lead. Perhaps Jenny could help Jimmy sort things out for you."

Emily studies the muffin in her hand as if hoping to see Jenny appear in it.

"How?" she finally asks.

"Well... when you've finished staring at that delicious muffin, and put it where it belongs, in your tummy, we could go over the Schubert Fantasy together whilst Jimmy and Jenny get to know each other."

And so, with muffins in tummies, grandmother and

granddaughter sit side by side, at the dusty Steinway grand piano in the music room, to be joined by Schubert, leaving Emily's brother and Mabel's longstanding best friend forever to get to know each other before coming up with a plan.

A plan that might save the girl from endless torment at school... and from death.

Chapter Two

"So! You're Emily's big brother. Finally, we get to meet up."

Jenny glances at grandmother and granddaughter now discussing the music on the piano music rest, seemingly arguing over who should play primo and who, secondo. Emily wants to stick with primo as Lingling always likes to be down in the bass, but her granny is insisting she swap places for a change.

"It'll help you to empathise with your friend," says the old lady. "Understand her better."

"I just can't believe we came second last year with Debussy's '*En Bateau.*' Lingling and I were such good friends then."

"You both deserved *first* prize. Remember... I was there!"

"Okay. Let's swap places, but I can't see how this'll make Lingling like me again."

After switching places, grandmother and granddaughter enter the troubled mind that plagued Schubert's final years, and Emily soon discovers how right her granny has been. It isn't all scary darkness down there in the lower octaves. There are moments of joy and of humour. The same feelings she used to experience when hanging out with her friends at school. Before...

...Before Belinda!

"My dear friend, Mabel, was always so right about

everything," Jenny says. "Let's leave them to get on with the music, Jimmy. Good opportunity to find out more about that Chinese girl, Lingling."

"You mean...?" begins Jimmy.

"I do, indeed!" agrees Jenny.

"But I've never..."

"Never travelled outside Emily? What with being her big brother, and all?"

"Guess we never saw the need."

"And she was thinking about killing herself? Shame on you!"

"Is it... you know... kind of creepy? I mean for me and Emily to be separated. Will I still exist?"

"You've heard her say so many times how real you are. Just that others can't see or hear you. Look, I may look like a teenager, but I've been around for well over seventy years. Learned a lot. I helped your granny get to where she is. Become what she became. One of the greatest pianists of the last century. Just stick with me and, whatever happens, do not panic. Remember... no one, apart from Emily, can see you."

"I wish Emily could see *you*. I think you're gorgeous!"

"Watch it! No time for all that lubby-dubby stuff."

"Would she know? If I've gone."

"Of course she would. You're inside her. Like a part of her. But we can wait till tomorrow. When she meets up with Lingling at school. Meanwhile..." Jenny offers Jimmy her elbow, grinning. "We stick together and get to know each other. But absolutely no funny business.

Remember, I'm seventy-seven."

"Worst luck!" mutters Jimmy, also grinning.

"Is there anything more you can tell me about Lingling? Other than that she's Chinese."

"Came to London two years ago. From Hong Kong. With her mum. Got some sort of a music scholarship."

"Is she good?"

"I know absolutely nothing about classical music. More into rap myself..."

"Jabber, jabber, jabber! And you call that music?"

"Yeah! It's got beat, man. And soul."

"Hmm! How does your little sister put up with you?"

"'Cos I'm the greatest! And way more handsome than—"

"Shut up! Lingling... tell me more."

Arms linked, they leave Emily and her granny in the soulful company of Franz Schubert and stroll out through the closed back door into a small, tidy little garden where, seated together on a bench, Jimmy tells Jenny what little he knows about Lingling.

*****

After sitting down next to Lingling, who did no more than briefly glance at her, Emily took out her iPad and sheets of mathematical equations from her school bag before placing it under her chair.

"Wish I had your brain," she whispered. "For me, maths is a total nightmare."

Lingling's only response was a slight shrug of her shoulders.

"You okay for a practice tonight?"

"Maybe," whispered the Chinese girl. "Depends on what Belinda has planned."

Which Emily took to mean, 'No!'

*****

"Well," begins Jimmy, "as always, Emily was the first to approach Lingling when she came to the school two years ago. They soon became real mates. Loved the same sort of music. Never out of each other's company at school and met up together every weekend. Not only to play music on Emily's piano. Went to the playground in the park. Joked about, and got teased by, the boys. Lingling's really pretty, you know. In an oriental kind of way. The boys took to her. As they would to–"

Jimmy attempts to take hold of Jenny's hand, but she quickly pulls it away.

"Like I said, 'No!' Look, just tell me more about Lingling the girl. What she's like. Apart from being Chinese and pretty. Her parents. Background. Anything!"

"Well, I do know it's just her and her mum. Her dad's still in Hong Kong. Work, I guess. Dunno what he's into. Triads?"

"Don't make fun of her dad, Jimmy. So... does she get on with her mum?"

Jimmy wipes a little collection of crumbs off his trousers. *Must have got there when Emily had one of granny's muffins,* he reckons. A thought occurs to him. If he and Jenny leave their real-life sister and friend behind, will he get to taste muffins himself? And chocolate cake and spaghetti carbonara that Emily so raves about?

"Well? Does she? Get on with her mum?"

"Dunno! Emily never went round to *her* place. It was always the other way around. When they were friends. And my sister's so generous, she never questioned why it was always *her* doing the entertaining. Countless sleepovers at our place, but never Lingling's."

"And you didn't think to ask yourself, 'Why not?' You're supposed to be her big brother!"

"Just that... well, I know next to nothing about girls."

"And you come from inside one?"

"Not now! I'm on my own, guys! Plus, *she* can be my imaginary sister. The other way around, for a change."

"Stop wittering, Jimmy. We've work to do. Tomorrow we'll join Emily and Lingling at school. I take it they still sit together in class, whatever Belinda says or does."

"True."

"Then tomorrow will be your first step into the unknown. Across the divide."

"Divide?"

"Between different realities. And..."

"And?"

"How's your Greek?"

"Emily likes Greek yoghurt."

"I'm talking more than yoghurt, chum. Hippocampus."

"Yeah, I saw one of those when I went with Emily and Lingling to the London Zoo one weekend. Great big, lazy, fat bugger, it was. Huge teeth though, so I kept quiet. Didn't want Emily to get bitten by it."

"Hippo*campus*, not hippo*potamus*! It's that part of the brain where memories are stored. Lingling's memories. As we're not real for Lingling, we can travel there unnoticed and find out who she really is, this girl who pretends to no longer be Emily's friend. Because of Belinda."

Chapter Three

"You don't have to whisper," Jenny says to Jimmy as Emily sits down next to Lingling in class the following morning. "Remember, you're only real for Emily, but she'll not be hearing you when she's busily occupied in their world. As soon as Lingling turns around, just follow me. Into her eyes. The back of each eye connects directly to the brain where we'll make our way to the hippocampus. And no, it won't bite like a hippopotamus. Think of it as a railway station. To take us to places in Lingling's past. Like going on a rail journey."

"Have you done this before?" asks Jimmy.

"Like I told you, I'm seventy-seven. So, there's not much I haven't done before. If you..." Lingling turns to face Emily and Jenny holds her breath.

"Sorry couldn't make Schubert practice at the weekend," says Lingling. "Belinda invited me round to Kami's with her."

"Now!" urges Jenny, in silence. She grabs Jimmy's arm, and together, unseen, they take a running jump at, and into, the Chinese girl's face. A quick scramble up the girl's pale cheek, then..."

"Wow!" exclaims Jimmy. "I thought it would be all dark and dingy in here, but it's really quite bright."

"Think different dimensions, Jimmy. Now, if I'm right, the hippocampus will be somewhere in..." Jenny circles around in different directions, for inside the girl's brain there is no 'up' nor 'down'. Jimmy wonders whether it would be much the same if he were an electron whizzing about inside a computer looking for an app. Not that being inside Emily taught him much about IT other than switching things on and off.

"There, in that direction!" suggests Jenny, pointing up and to his left.

"Game for anything!" says Jimmy, more to quell his mounting anxiety that perhaps getting inside Lingling's young and active brain is not such a good idea after all. He has an uneasy feeling that this is a first for Jenny, too.

He follows Jenny through a kaleidoscope of ever-changing, colourful patterns, soon forgetting his fear. *Unbelievably beautiful*, he thinks, and cannot help but wonder whether he, too, has a similar weirdly wonderful world inside his own head. He can hardly wait to tell his sister all about it, but, according to Jenny, what he tells the girl must depend on what they find in Lingling's hippocampus.

Not hippopotamus!

"Over there!" announces Jenny. "Hong Kong, here we come!"

*****

"What do you mean, Baba[1]'s in trouble?" Lingling asked her mother in English. She preferred to speak in English now that she was heavily into Western music that she so adored. Baba, coming from the mainland,

---

[1] 'Daddy' in Chinese

wanted her to learn the *erhu*[2], but she went on so about it sounding like a mosquito being tortured that he desisted, and finally agreed to her having piano lessons.

"You know about those things happening in the streets, Lingling?" the girl's mother asked.

"The demonstrations? To keep Hong Kong 'special', like before? Different from Mainland China?"

"Your baba came here to escape what he calls the 'communist devils'. It's how we met, Baba and me. And now the devils, they come here anyway. To take away our freedom. Our rights. Our independence."

"So?" queried Lingling. "Why is Baba in trouble?"

Tears welled in her mother's eyes. Somehow these told the girl what she needed to know. That her father was in prison. Already, she knew this meant she might never see him again.

"I so tried to warn him, Lingling. To say nothing. Or even tell lies. Like say that he loves Xi Jinping. But you know your father. Only ever tells the truth. Here, and now, truth can be so dangerous."

Lingling took hold of her mother's hands.

"Baba told me something last week," she said. "When I heard about me getting that music scholarship. If anything happened to him, 'Go straight to the British Consulate,' he said. 'There's a man there called, erm...'"

"Mr Hayes?"

"Yes! That's it. Mr Hayes. Baba said he'll look after us. Because of my scholarship. We can go to London.

---

[2] Two-stringed Chinese musical instrument

16

We *must*. Like we'd planned to do, together with Baba, only—"

The girl's mother reverted to Cantonese (which, being inside Lingling, Jimmy understood) after the girl began to sob...

"Only they took Baba away yesterday. And I can't get in touch with him. Mobile turned off all the time. Police say they know nothing."

"Now!" said Lingling in Cantonese. "We must leave now. Before they come for you, too. Asking questions. I really don't want to end up in an orphanage. A girl at school said they feed you smelly dead rats in those places and beat you with a stick. And I'd never again play the piano. I..."

The doorbell rang, followed by a series of frenzied thumps on the door.

"No!" shrieked Lingling.

Thankfully, Mrs Lau's voice called out, half-drowned by her thumping,

"The police are outside in the street. You must hide with me. Quick!" their trustworthy neighbour shouted.

Lingling ran to open the door, for her mother seemed frozen in a state of shock. Mrs Lau pulled the girl out onto the landing and pushed her into her humble apartment adjacent to the Tans'.

"Our things? Passports... money?" protested Mrs Tan, Lingling's mother, who followed.

"No time, no time."

They heard the hum of the elevator in action whilst, firmly, Mrs Lau dragged her neighbour into her own apartment to join the woman's daughter before slamming the front door behind them just as the elevator door slid open.

"Quiet!" warned Mrs Lau as she did some quick-thinking before herding the mother and daughter into a clothes cupboard where they were told to crouch down before the woman covered them with blankets and clothes.

Huddled together, petrified, and barely daring to breathe, Lingling and her mum listened to the muffled conversation outside Mrs Lau's apartment. Jabbering in Cantonese, followed by banging on the door of their apartment, then, after a brief pause, a loud, splintering crash. Their front door had been broken open. The only comfort for Lingling was that she couldn't hear any dogs. Dogs, and they would be doomed.

Soon, the banging started up again. On the door of Mrs Lau's apartment. Their neighbour calmly opened the door, and, cool as an ice cube, asked the officers whether she could be of any help.

"Mrs Tan and her daughter? Have you seen them? Do you know where they might be?"

Lingling gritted her teeth, praying to the Lord Buddha that they would not be betrayed. Her father was a devout believer although she, herself, had doubts about there being about any power on Earth or Heaven that could stand up to the Chinese Communist Party.

"She left half an hour ago," replied Mrs Lau to the police out on the landing. "Seemed in a hurry. Making a lot of noise, so I popped my head out of the door and told her to keep quiet. I was trying to get some sleep. All those stupid demonstrations are doing my head in. Why don't you lot do your job and put them all in jail? Or send them to the Mainland?"

Lingling heard laughter from one of the officers. It reminded the girl of a dentist's drill, boring into her skull. But she secretly blessed Mrs Lau for, after a brief exchange of shared views about the anti-Chinese activities of those demonstrators ('devils', Mrs Lau called them), the front door closed. Quietness resumed.

"Can we trust our neighbour?" whispered Mrs Tan to her daughter. "Those things she was saying out there. About your father and the other demonstrators."

"Of course, Mama. Why would she hide us if she's not to be trusted?"

The cupboard door opened. Lightness returned. Blankets and clothes were pulled away to reveal Mrs Lau's cheerful, grinning face.

"The devils are gone. But they'll be back, for sure.
"Where—?"

"British Consulate!" interrupted Lingling. "Baba told me."

"No passports?"

Lingling shrugged her shoulders. Her mother was still in a state of stunned shock, so the girl took over.

"No matter. We just have to get there. And ask for a Mr Hayes. He knows my father."

"I have an idea," offered Mrs Lau. "Chickens. *Live* chickens."

"What?" asked Lingling.

19

"My brother-in-law. Micky Chiu. He delivers live chickens to some of the embassies early every morning. The British, they love their chickens, he says. They've no idea how to cook them properly, but that doesn't matter. I'll take you down to where he keeps them, and you can hide amongst the chickens. Till tomorrow morning. Wait–"

Mrs Lau disappeared into her kitchen, soon returning with a bag containing a bottle of water and some *bao buns*[3].

"These should keep you going till tomorrow. And just pee with the chickens. They won't mind."

"Yuk!" exclaimed Lingling.

Both carrying sunshades, supposedly to keep out the sun, but really to hide their faces, Lingling and her mother left their apartment block and followed Mrs Lau, sticking to narrow side streets away from the crowds and the police, with no possessions other than a bottle of water and a few bao buns. Contented clucking signalled their arrival at Micky Chiu's chicken storage facility beside the water. They saw a line of chicken coops. Micky, the chicken guy, appeared from out of one of these on hearing his sister-in-law call out. After listening to a brief explanation for their presence, he herded the mother and daughter into a coop, grinning, before securing the door. Squashed, side-by-side, on the floor, at the far end of the coop, Lingling and her mother sat backs up against the wall and tried to make

---

3 Pronounced 'bow', steamed Chinese buns or 'baozi'

sense of what was happening to their lives.

"Poor Lingling," whispers Jimmy.

"What did you just say, Mama?" asked Lingling.

Jimmy bites his lip whilst Jenny holds a finger to her lips. No longer is he only real for Emily.

"Nothing," replied Mrs Tan. "It must have been the chickens you heard,"

Thankfully, Lingling seemed to like animals, including birds. She almost giggled when one of the chickens came up close, cocked her head to one side to study mother and daughter with a solitary eye, then uttered chickenlike contentment in a series of clucks as though giving the human intruders her approval.

Or maybe she was politely asking for one of the *bao buns*?

Inside Lingling's hippocampus, Jimmy and Jenny remained with the Chinese girl and her mother all night, aware that neither was able to sleep a wink. Mr Chiu arrived back at first light, grabbing squawking chickens and pushing them into crates. He handed a couple of overalls to the girl and the woman and told them to 'gown-up and look busy.' He reassured Lingling (her mother remained uncommunicatively silent) that no one would suspect a couple of his workers of being escaping would-be refugees. At the British Consulate, they were to deliver a crate of live chickens and say that Mr Chiu told them he needed to speak with a certain Mr Hayes.

As they climbed into his truck, Lingling told her mother to let *her* do all the talking.

"My English is better," she explained, although, in truth, Jimmy knows this isn't the real reason for the girl to wish to take control. Suddenly, instead of hating Lingling for joining Belinda's bunch of bullies that were making his sister's life at school a total nightmare, he has enormous respect for her.

They arrived at the British Consulate in no time at all and were dropped off at the door. The woman who opened the door to receive a pair of noisy chickens (their British head-though-useless-chef insisted on 'live', Mr Chiu had informed them) seemed to understand the plight of Lingling and her mother even before the girl, in a garbled outpouring, begged to see a certain 'Mr Hayes' because 'it's so very important." After what seemed an age, but in truth little more than a few minutes, a balding, grey-moustachioed gentleman appeared and quickly ushered the mother and daughter inside the building, closing the door behind them. And before she could even open her mouth, Mr Hayes said he knew all about Lingling and her mother and had been expecting them.

"You know my father?" Lingling asked.

"Know and worked with," came the reply. "Your dad's one of us, so to speak. But the less said the better. So you, Lingling, are the gifted pianist. With a scholarship. A bursary for that private girls' school in London with a reputation for music. Come with me. And don't look at anyone. Even here, I don't know whom to trust."

With Jenny and Jimmy watching as if glued to a

Hollywood movie, Lingling and her mother followed the suited English gentleman upstairs, along a corridor into a small and very ordinary-looking office. Mr Hayes closed the door behind him.

"We have nothing," said Lingling. "No papers, no passport..."

The man held up his hand to silence her.

"No matter. Your father and I have it all worked out. Sit down."

He indicated two chairs in front of a desk. Lingling and her mother complied. Mr Hayes pulled open the desk drawer, took out a large buff envelope and tipped its contents onto the desk top. Amongst some papers and envelopes were two passports.

"You, Mrs Tan, are Angela Chang travelling to the United Kingdom to visit your sister, Zhang Minling, who runs a Chinese restaurant in Bradford. And you, Lingling, are Li Jingchen. English name Maxine. Flying as an unaccompanied minor. A music scholar. Do not worry. You are booked on the same flight, but not sitting together. Just in case, though I expect you will be leaving the secret police behind at the airport. The Chinese aren't like the Russians who have their spies everywhere. But do take care at the airport here in Hong Kong. Remember. You do not know each other. Lingling will be looked after by British Airways. As an unaccompanied minor, 'Maxine Li'."

For a few moments Lingling and her mother just looked at each other before collapsing into a tearful hug.

Jimmy saw Mr Hughes explain the various documents laid out on his desk before handing a mobile phone to each of his two charges. He told them how they would be met, separately, at Heathrow Airport, then taken to the same hotel in Government vehicles. Finally, he asked whether they trusted him. Lingling spoke quickly in Cantonese to her mother, who nodded, before nodding, herself, at the stranger who now had complete control over their lives. What other choice did the poor girl have, Jimmy wonders?

Jimmy and Jenny see the mother and daughter taken to a twin bedroom on the top floor of the Consulate. Jimmy closes his eyes whilst Lingling undresses. No way could he have Emily accuse him of being a peeping Tom, but he has to end up with his hands forcibly covering his eyes which keep trying to persuade him to open them. He'll have to own up to his sister that he does find Chinese girls attractive.

Emily's brother realises that time within Lingling's hippocampus behaves differently to the fourth dimension of Emily's real world. In *no* time, he and Jenny are watching Lingling, or Maxine as she was now called, being taken, alone, by taxi, to Hong Kong International Airport. He prays that Mr Hayes is honest, and that Mrs Tan is in another taxi heading in the same direction. Then, quite suddenly, the 'movie' switches off. Voices appear in his head. Angry voices. Calming voices. One starts to hum a tune. It sounds weirdly oriental.

"Trust Mr Hayes," said a man's voice as three-dimensional, coloured zig-zags zip across Jimmy's field of vision. Yet, does he *really* see these things? Seems more as though he feels them. Smells them, even.

Quite suddenly, Mrs Tan reappeared, and Jimmy was back in that little apartment in Hong Kong; the woman was searching through drawers, cupboards and cardboard boxes laid out tall over the floor. Was she looking for Lingling? Jimmy wants to call out and tell the woman to make haste to the airport for they have a flight to catch. A flight to safety. A flight towards a new life for Lingling. But he knows he doesn't exist for her, and in the real world, neither does she, for all of this is happening in her daughter's hippocampus.

A monotonous hum. An airplane engine. There sat Lingling, fear imprinted on her eyes, staring vacantly at an inflight movie playing on the screen in front of her. To Jimmy's great relief, the girl's mother was seated on the other side of the aisle a few rows back. Almost without blinking, she kept her daughter in her line of vision. Jimmy breathes a sigh of relief. Mr Hayes is to be trusted. But what did he mean by, 'Mr Tan is one of us'? A spy working for British Security in China? How dangerous could that be?

Cut... plane gone. Chickens re-appeared. Lingling giggled. She and her mother climbed into Mr Chiu's chicken truck. Again. Or not. Memories came and went, over and over, often merging with those colourful, flickering lines, until...

"Mama, we'll be all right. Baba has made sure of it. You heard what that lady from the new school said.

She'll get me fitted up with a school uniform tomorrow whilst the woman who met us at Heathrow Airport takes you clothes shopping and lets you into our new apartment."

Another 'movie'. Mother and daughter were sitting side by side in a hotel foyer.

"Lingling, you are truly your father's daughter! He'd be so proud of you," Mrs Tan said. An attempt at reassurance that had the reverse effect. The girl collapsed sideways onto her mother's shoulder, sobbing uncontrollably. Mrs Tan stroked her long, sleek, black hair before resting an arm across her daughter's shoulders...

Jimmy has seen enough.

"Let's go. Now!" he whispers to Jenny. "Emily has to know the truth."

Chapter Four

Granny always makes Emily feel so much better. Did the girl seriously want to kill herself? She'll never know. Only that with Jimmy inside her, and with Granny out there, in the Vale of Health, death is no longer an option. Somehow, together, they always seem to give Emily the strength to try again. And again, and again until...

Until Belinda drops dead?

No, Jimmy wouldn't want that. Not his way. This much, Emily does know about her brother. But why, this Monday morning, does he keep appearing in her head? Like there's something he so desperately wants to tell her. She didn't drown herself last weekend, so isn't that enough for him? Besides, Monday is always far too busy for brother-sister head-to-heads.

"Tomorrow!" she says to Jimmy whilst sorting out her locker at school.

"Talking to yourself again, Emily?" Belinda holds up her smart phone having just recorded the other girl, apparently speaking to herself, for Snapchat. "Must put this around! Perhaps..." She comes up close to Emily who, with her locker door open, steps back whilst resting her right hand on the locker shelf. "Perhaps someone should invent an app for weirdos. Freakchat?"

As Belinda, laughing at her own wit, passes Emily, her head held high, she appears to stumble, on purpose, crashing into the locker door which slams   against

Emily's trapped hand.

"Ow!" screams Emily, grabbing her injured hand. The pain must be excruciating, for howling, she slumps to the floor, frantically nursing her hand. It nudges aside all that mental pain of the bullying, tearing at every fibre in her body.

Jimmy tries to comfort her...

"Sis, you'll be all right. I'm sure nothing's broken."

But he isn't sure. And Emily is certain of only one thing. No way will she be able to enter the North London Festival of Music and Drama Competition with Lingling the following month. Even if she is able to play the piano again by then, practice sessions are off the agenda for the foreseeable future.

"Belinda did that deliberately. You cannot let her get away with it," Jimmy insists.

"She already has!" Emily says aloud.

"Emily? Who are you talking about? Look, I just saw that Snapchat thing on my phone..."

Lingling is standing in front of Emily, peering down at her. She pauses, for she quickly realises the other girl is in great pain.

"Are you okay?" she asks. "And what are you doing on the floor?"

Tears streaming, and holding her hand, Emily looks up at the Chinese girl. She says nothing as Lingling crouches down and gently takes hold of Emily's hand. Jimmy is virtually screaming inside Emily's head, urging her to tell Lingling the truth about what happened, but his sister seems to have lost all the fight left in her. He had been so pleased to see her remarkable turnaround whilst with their granny the day before, but now it seems as though she's fallen back into a bleak, bottomless hole.

Lingling helps Emily up and, supporting her, takes her along to the caretaker's office. Mr Crawford, a gentle soul who can always be relied upon *never* to report any misdemeanors, gets the girl to sit down whilst he examines her injured hand.

"How?" he asks, a man of few words.

"Caught in the locker door," is the sobbed answer.

"Hmm!" the man grunts, looking accusingly back at Lingling.

"Not me!" the Chinese girl insists, but she has already put two and two together. That brief footage, taken by Belinda, on Snapchat, then this? It has to be.

"Hospital!" says Mr Crawford. "X-ray. Painkillers. Skin's broken, too. Needs cleaning up. By professionals."

"I'll go with her," Lingling chips in.

Thank goodness, thinks Jimmy. *Emily and Lingling alone together at long last. We'll do it!*

"Do what?" says Emily, unsure who has spoken those words in her head.

"I'll come with you," insists Lingling. "That's what I'll do."

"Good idea," agrees Mr Crawford, reaching into his pocket. "Here." He produces a set of keys. "Take Emily to the school minibus. Parked out the front. Wait for me. I'll let Mrs Gray know what's happened."

"My mum. She'll be in the surgery. She's a GP. She can—"

"No! Hospital. X-ray. See you both in the minibus."

Without further ado, Lingling takes Emily, still sobbing, out to the minibus and a short while later the girls, together with Jimmy, are on their way to the hospital. They are left at Accident & Emergency whilst Mr Crawford drives off to find a parking space, and Lingling accompanies Emily to a cubicle where she is quickly attended to by a nurse, then by a doctor who agrees that an X-ray is called for.

Thankfully, no bones are broken. Emily's hand is cleansed and dressed. She is given some painkillers and a sling and within an hour they are on their way back to the school.

"Now's the time," Jimmy whispers to his sister. "To tell Lingling that you know what she's been through. That you understand about her father and that our parents can help find out what's happened to him. I know everything! Let me do the prompting."

"How do you know?" responds Emily, silently, frowning.

"Been inside her head if you must know. With Granny's imaginary friend, Jenny. Gorgeous, she is, but, sadly, seventy-seven. We ended up in a place, inside Lingling's brain, called the hippocampus. Bursting with memories. And we saw it all. Like watching a movie."

"Aren't the painkillers working, Emily? You've got such a frown on your face, I wish I could do something more," says Lingling.

"Hardly hurting at all, now. No, it's something my brother told me."

"I didn't know you had a brother."

"Big brother..." Emily pauses. "He's away most of the time. Look, he has access to certain information."

"What information?"

Lingling's turn to frown. Can she trust the other girl, she seems to be thinking?

And so, it all comes out. That Emily (or rather, her big brother hidden away inside her) knows what Lingling went through in Hong Kong. She knows all about the demonstrations, of course, because the Television News is full of them, but she also knows that Mr Tan was taken away by the secret police and neither Lingling nor her mum have any information about him. The Chinese girl stares vacantly ahead, in disbelief, whilst listening to what Emily is telling her. When the other girl is finished, and she's staring at nothing in particular in front of her, and Jimmy-inside-Emily has gone silent whilst waiting for a response, Lingling speaks:

"Who *is* this brother of yours that no one knows anything about?"

"He saved my life."

Lingling turns to look at Emily. She can see, in her friend's eyes, that the girl is telling the truth.

"Has he told anyone else? About my baba—my dad—being in prison?"

"Of course not. How can he? No one else can see or

hear him."

"Belinda's always said you're weird."

"It's true, isn't it? About your dad?"

Lingling nods. Then unpredictably, just when Emily expects the Chinese girl to slap her because she seems so upset, Lingling puts her arm around her and hugs her.

"She's so cruel," is all she says, clearly referring to Belinda, as the minibus turns into the school driveway.

Chapter Five

Jimmy high fives with Jenny.

"One down," he says. "Four to go! Excluding Belinda, of course."

"What?" questions Jenny, preoccupied looking at the other girls in the school as they follow Emily and Lingling to their classroom. It's mid-morning break, and most students are hanging around in the corridor, in pairs, or groups, many glued to their smart phones. "This is kind of weird. Their skirts are so short it's like they've nothing on. In my day they'd all get sent home to dress properly."

"Nothing wrong with a short skirt. You should try one on," suggests Jimmy, grinning. "Bet you've got nice legs!"

"Watch it! So, what did you mean by 'One down, four to go'?"

"Belinda's other so-called friends. The ones she stole from Emily. Well, five more including *her*. The 'Beast' I'd like to call her, but Emily doesn't like me using names like that. You know, I've never once known my sister be unkind about anyone. Why do they all pick on her?"

"It was the same with Mabel."

"My granny? Really?"

"Uh-huh!"

"Tell me more about Granny. She's always so helpful. Can't believe other kids had it in for her when she was little."

"Ah... but she was *different* from them, see."

"In what way?"

"Let's find somewhere quiet to talk about her. Too noisy to think here. We should follow Emily and Lingling into their classroom. Must be where they're heading. Break time, so it'll be empty."

In the classroom, as Emily and Lingling sit together, sharing sorrows, Jimmy listens intently to Jenny's version of his granny's troubled life as a Cockney child in North London.

"She was probably the only person, apart from one old man, within a radius of five miles of their ground floor flat in a row of terraced houses, who loved classical music, and she always struggled to understand why this should make her stand out as being 'weird'. Plus, just like her granddaughter, she would always come out with whatever appeared in her head. No filtering of words to suit whoever might be listening to her. And local adult female gossipmongers saw to it that the whole neighbourhood, which included other local state school kids, knew all about the 'other' family in Newcastle. She was teased mercilessly, whatever she said or did, but found so much comfort in music that, whenever alone, she would play the piano inside her head and escape into another world.

"An old fellow up the road had a piano. One day, when the man's wife saw a seven-year-old Mabel standing outside, listening intently to the music emerging from their house, she asked the girl in.

"Her husband had been a music teacher in a local boy's school, Mabel told me, and was more than happy to give the little girl piano lessons for free on hearing that Mabel's parents weren't well off. Amazed by the Cockney child's musical talent, the kind old guy allowed her free access to his piano anytime she wanted to play it. Which soon became every evening and most of every weekend. Within five years, she was tackling the late Beethoven sonatas not only with technical brilliance, but a degree of musical understanding rare in some of the most gifted internationally recognised pianists.

"When he first introduced her to his grand piano, Mr Honey proudly informed Mabel it was a Bechstein, and that Brahms himself played a Bechstein. Mabel had no idea who Brahms was, or had been, but later, when she learned to play the composer's intermezzi on the same instrument, knowing that he, too, played a Bechstein seemed to add depth to her performance.

"The young Mabel was soon playing at a totally different level to her ageing teacher. Mr Honey had no hard feelings about this. Finally, after a lifetime of teaching music, he had a true musician under his wing. He and Mrs Honey had no children themselves, and Mabel became like a surrogate daughter for them. Her own mother's bouts of depression, and her father's long and frequent absences from the (London) family home helped in this respect. And as her 'surrogate father', the old music teacher felt duty bound to buy her an upright Steinway...

"*You, young lady, will be wanting to perform on a*

Steinway for all those grand concerts across the world in the future', I heard him tell her. Plus, of course, there was paid tuition from top pianists at the Royal College of Music until, at the age of sixteen, she became a piano student herself.

"The rest, you know. One of the greatest pianists of the last century, many folk reckon."

*****

"Can I meet this brother of yours?" asks Lingling. "There's so much I want to ask him."

Emily can hardly own up to the fact that Jimmy has already been inside her friend's hippocampus.

"He's not around just now," she lies. "But is there anything special you want to know? I do talk to him most days."

"Can he get in touch with Mr Hayes in Hong Kong? They said we mustn't contact anyone there. Communist spies might come looking for me. Particularly as I no longer call myself Maxine 'Whatsit' like it says on my passport. Lingling Tan. They'll know who I am. Maybe come and get me and Mum." Emily looks thoughtful. "I'll help you with Belinda and the gang," promises Lingling.

"Not that easy," responds Emily. Then, changing the subject, she says, "Look, there's no way I can play the piano till my hand's better. Why don't I get you to come and meet my granny? Practise the Schubert with her. "

"With the famous pianist?" the Chinese girl questions excitedly.

"She's still pretty good, though not able to give concerts any more. We'll pretend we're at the Festival, and I can be piano duet section judge."

Lingling pulls a funny face.

"Don't be too hard on me!" she says.

Emily laughs for the first time in a very long while.

"I'll try not to be," she replies. "But I'll tell you one thing. Granny's got friends all over the world. Because of who she is. Played many times in Hong Kong. Connections, aye?"

Emily grins at Lingling who gives her a hug.

"No way will Belinda get away with this. I'm accompanying Kami on the piano this evening. I'll tell her how kind you've been. She's also a great Schubert fan."

"I know. We used to play the Schubert violin sonatinas together, her and me. Until—"

"Yeah! Until Belinda appeared. Kami's not been herself at all, recently. I'll try to find out why. Then see if you and Jimmy could help her, too, like you've helped me."

"Not exactly helped. More like understood."

"That's sort of helping. Can't wait to meet your famous granny. Will Jimmy be able to come too?"

"Too dangerous!"

"What?"

"He might fall in love with you."

Lingling laughs.

"I've no time for boys!" she says without conviction.

"Famous last words. Oops... Kami's outside in the

corridor. Heard her voice. Just pretend you're looking at my hand. And don't mention Belinda."

"Why not? She did this to you. And to *me*, if you're not better for the Festival next month."

"Jimmy told me not to. Not yet. Just say it's an accident."

Kami enters the classroom followed by Belinda. Lingling, holding Emily's injured hand, looks up.

"Emily caught her hand in her locker door," she says. "An accident. I went with her to A & E. Mr Crawford took us."

"Wondered where you'd got to, Lingling," remarks Belinda as though Emily isn't there.

Kami comes up close to look at Emily's bandaged hand.

"Can you play with it?" she asks.

"What do you think?" the other girl replies.

"Oh dear, oh dear!" exclaims Belinda. She walks over to the window to look out just as the school bell rings. "All that fame and glory out the window, ay?"

Kami ignores her.

"I'm so sorry, Emily," she says looking straight into Emily's eyes brimming with tears again.

"Now!" urges Jenny, giving Jimmy a nudge. "Quick. Follow me into Kami's eyes."

"And her hippopotamus?" jokes Jimmy.

"Shut up! And be careful. Can't have you getting lost and just becoming a distant memory somewhere inside the brain of Emily's violin-playing friend."

Chapter Six

"**Nice** shade of blue, ay?" says Jimmy as they zip backwards along an optic nerve to enter the girl's brain."

"What's blue?"

"Kami's eyes. Fabulous colour."

"I thought you had the hots for the Chinese girl."

"No! You heard! It's *she* who wants to meet up with *me*."

"In your dreams. Now, pay attention. Hey, that sound..."

"A violin?"

"Coming from...?"

As before, Jenny circles in all directions trying to decide from which direction the sound of a violin is coming. "Definitely from... erm..." she looks up. "There!" she announces, pointing upwards.

"This is so different," Jimmy observes. "I mean, last time it was all colourful zigzags and twirls, but now—"

"Just..." Jenny frowns, deciding what word to describe what they both clearly felt. "More kind of...?"

"Touch?" offers Jimmy. "Like we're being stroked. Or fondled. Or...? No, it's a smell. Definitely odorous, though I can also feel it. Yuk! Stinky!"

"Hurry," interrupts Jenny, grabbing Jimmy by the arm before pulling him upwards. Up and up and up, towards the soulful sound of an unaccompanied violin.

"Think I prefer the—" Jimmy is about to say 'piano'

when Jenny comes to a sudden halt. Rather, she bumps into a door, in the dark, across which muffled, sad strains of solo violin music seem to cry out for help.

"Stay quiet," instructs Jenny as her free, searching hand circles, in darkness, over the door till it makes contact with a handle. "Not a peep from you, Jimmy. It could be dangerous. I've got a *bad* feeling about this place."

"Dangerous? Why?" whispers Jimmy. "How many people d'you know who have been killed by a violin? Mind you, I heard Emily once say that a badly played fiddle was enough to make anyone want to commit suicide."

"Quiet! We're going through. As we're not real for whoever's inside that room, they'll not be aware of us.""

Slowly, Jenny opens the door. Brightness suddenly fills the space they're in, and, invisible to the girl seated on her bed, violin and bow in her confident hands, they enter what is clearly a girl's bedroom. A large poster of a handsome young pop star, mouth open, electric guitar in his hands, half fills one wall. On a chair, in a corner of the room, sits a soft toy kangaroo. The top of a chest of drawers with a mirror is littered with make-up items and, on a desk opposite, lies an open violin case. The bed is strewn with clothes which spill over onto the floor, and amongst these sits Kami in her underwear.

"Close your eyes," whispers Jenny.

"Nope! Seen it all before. With Emily. But what's she doing playing the violin in her underwear?"

"Chilling out, I guess. Wait... there's someone

outside."

Jenny holds a finger to her lips as the bedroom door opened...

A young man appeared in the doorway. He was only wearing a shirt. No trousers. The girl put the violin down on the bed beside her, and looked up at the man, little more than early twenties at the most. She appeared terrified beyond words.

"Don't stop," he said. "I like it. Matches your Cami knickers. Just like your name, my little violin-playing sister."

"Please, Mark. Not now. No more. I need to–"

"*You* need to be nice to me, sis. You know what we do to naughty little girls who aren't nice in my church."

Mark entered the bedroom and closed the door behind him.

"Our loving parents are away on an anniversary dinner date, as you well know, so we have all the time in the world to let God into our dull little lives."

Jimmy turns, horrified, to look at Jenny. She, too, is frowning. They share the same thought. To rush forward, grab the young man who is clearly Kami's big brother, and eject him from the privacy of the girl's bedroom. But they can't, for what they witness is merely a memory of something that actually happened. As Jenny told Emily's brother earlier, there are no fantasies in the hippocampus. Only pure, unadulterated truths.

Mark points to the instrument beside his young sister.

"Well, you'll not be needing that just now, will you, Knickers, much as I love to hear you play the violin? Bach, was it?"

"Knickers?" whispers Jimmy. "As in 'Cami'? Is that what he calls his sister? What an arsehole!"

In slow motion, the girl, reaching over the side of her bed, carefully placed the violin on the floor. Then she got up and removed the strewn clothes before smoothing the bedspread. Her brother laid himself down on the bed, like a lord of the manor, then beckoned to his sister to join him. Jimmy watches in frozen horror as the girl meekly complied with his demands, lying stiffly down beside him. She remained rigid with fear, for Jimmy sees this in her eyes, as Mark took hold of her hand and gave it a squeeze.

"Remember what I said the last the time we were together like this?" the brother said. His sister merely nodded. "That you must remain virgo intacta. For God. And for me, because soon, little sister, I shall be a man of God. Not only you, but also our parents will have to look up to me. So..."

Mark turned over towards his sister, stroked her cheek, then rested his hand on her cleavage above her bra.

"I'll kill him," says Jimmy. "She's his sister, for God's sake. He should be protecting her from—"

With his other hand, Mark forced the girl to turn her face towards him. She was crying. He planted an unwanted kiss on her lips.

"Now you really don't want to be a naughty little girl

again, do you?" the brother said. "All these tears? I mean, if you refuse to let God into your life, I'll just have to put you across my knees again. Teach you a lesson like the last time, ay?" He stroked her cheek. Kami shook her head, as though being threatened by an unwelcome flying insect. "You wouldn't want me to redden that little bottom of yours once more, Knickers, would you?" Kami shook her head again and remained motionless as her brother fondled her and played with himself at the same time.

"We've seen enough," mutters Jimmy. "Please. Let's go. I must warn Emily. She *has* to do something about this."

Suddenly, darkness descended. Jenny and Jimmy are standing in a swirling grey mist. They're outside in a garden. A light flickers ahead. It grows brighter. A candle, held by a small girl; Kami, when she was much younger. Maybe ten or eleven. She was being tailed by her brother, also younger. Sixteen, at a guess. Both are in school uniform, heading towards an outhouse.

Hesitantly, the girl entered shed, the boy followed, closing the door behind him.

"Please don't!" the girl cried out.

"It's what happens to naughty little girls," the boy said. "I saw you both. Laughing together, coming back from school. You and that little lout Simon three doors up the road. D'you want me to tell our parents? Dad'll take away your annoying little pet rabbit if he knows you're walking home from school with him. Have the bunny put down, maybe."

"We did nothing wrong."

"That's why you need a good spanking to teach you the difference between right and wrong."

"It hurts," the girl protests.

The boy sat down on an upturned garden waste bin.

"Meant to. Now be a good little Knickers, lift up your skirt and get yourself across my knees."

Jimmy pulls at Jenny's arm.

"Now!" he insists. "Let's get out of here. Quick!"

As though a giant hoover was sucking them backwards, out of that terrifying darkness, Jimmy and Jenny find themselves back in that classroom, invisible to Emily, Kami and Lingling. Kami is still staring at Emily's injured hand.

"Your parents are both doctors, aren't they?" she says. "Surely they can make your hand better before the Festival Competition next month."

"They're not witchdoctors," Emily replies. "But you, Lingling. I can't let you down. Please. Come and practise the Schubert with my granny."

"I *can* play the piano," offers Kami. "Not like you guys, for sure, but I can play with Kami till you're recovered, Emily."

"Well, Granny might appreciate that, Kami. Her arthritis is pretty bad. But her piano's out of this world. And you and Lingling could play the sonatinas together as well if you bring your violin. Granny would love to hear you."

Gradually, the classroom fills up with students returning in twos and threes. All the while, Belinda

stands alone, looking out from the window at...
At what? Her own beautiful reflection?

Chapter Seven

Lunch time. Finally, Jimmy is able to speak with his sister alone, apart, that is, from Jenny who never leaves his side now that his granny has little need of her friendship. In fact, it's been difficult for Jenny ever since Mabel became famous and married her agent. Difficult responding to the need to find another 'invisible friend'. But that's a whole different story. As for Jenny, she never once felt let down by her friend Mabel. Only intensely proud of the impoverished Cockney girl whom she helped to become an internationally famous classical musician.

As always, Emily is sitting by herself, using her left hand to poke, with her fork, at a dangerously undercooked sausage.

"We have to talk," says Jimmy.

Emily looks up.

"What about?" she asks, grumpily. She told Lingling and Kami to stay away from her during lunch break, not wanting Belinda to turn on them as well. Try as she may, she cannot figure out why that girl with the face of Botticelli angel has it in for her.

"About Kami," answers Jimmy. "It's serious."

Emily looks around to check. There's no one looking at her. Normal. After all, thanks to the 'Gospel according to Belinda', she's to be avoided. A teaching followed, religiously, not only by all in her class, but, nowadays, also by most of the girls in the school.

"Let's talk in the toilet, Brother. Peace and quiet. Better than death by sausage, anyway."

With her big brother inside her, Emily leaves the dining room to hear, in the toilet, what he has to say that's so serious.

"So, what's this about Kami? She actually seemed to care about my hurt hand back then. Lingling too. She even wants to tell on Belinda, but I said, 'No way'. The big bully would only make things a thousand times worse. There were no witnesses, anyhow. She made sure of this before slamming that locker door on my hand."

"Nothing to do with Belinda, Emily. Kami's in trouble. Because of her big brother. He's going to be a priest, for God's sake!"

"A *baby* priest."

"Some priest! And certainly no 'baby'," asserted Jimmy. "He's abusing her."

"He's *what*?"

"Like I said. Abuse. *Sexual* abuse."

"A gonna-be priest molesting his little sister? You're having me on!"

"I'm as certain as the hard truth lurking in her hippocampus. Jenny and I took a ride via her optic nerves, and... I know you won't believe this, but what we saw made me actually feel like vomiting. Her parents were out, and he went into her bedroom half-dressed when she only had her underwear on whilst playing the violin, and he made her lie beside him as he... well, as he kind of pawed her all over and forced a kiss on her. On the lips. And threatened to spank her if she didn't go along with him. Plus, it was happening way back when she was still at primary school. He spanked her on the bottom one day for walking home from school with a boy called Simon. Said their parents would take away her pet rabbit if they knew. He's evil."

Shocked, at first Emily merely stares blankly ahead. Finally, she speaks:

"An evil priest? Oh my God!"

"Yeah! Seems to think he's God just because he's gonna be a priest. Emily, we've *got* to do something."

"You're right."

"Plus, I think you should come clean about me. Tell those two girls that, although I'm only real for you, I do exist. In another dimension. One that can link up with yours in what I like to call the 'memory trap'... though Jenny prefers that posh word, 'hippocampus'. Those memories we saw were definitely for real, and we have to help Kami before it's too late."

"Too late?"

"Before he rapes her."

"Sounds like he might've done that already."

"Don't think so. Mark... that's his name... he went on about her being 'virgo intacta' for 'God'. By which he means himself, of course."

"I think Lingling will understand. She so loves her own dad who's in prison in China, but she'll know only too well what bastards men can be."

"Not all of us are, Little Sister!"

"Tell you what, Big Brother... I'll invite them both

round to Granny's this weekend. But first, I'll talk to Mum. She's a doctor. She'll know how to play it. All righty?"

"If you say so," agrees Jimmy. "But it's an awful long wait till the weekend."

"Wednesday afternoon, then. I can't do sports with this injured hand. Lingling can use the Festival competition as an excuse. She can pretend Kami's offering to practise the Schubert with her instead of me. On Granny's piano. And Mum always has Wednesdays off. She can come as well."

"Sorted, then?"

"Not till that Mark's locked up and Lingling has her dad back. But it's a start. By the way, with my friends, do I call you 'Jimmy' or 'James'?"

"Jimmy. James is only for Kings. And ancient ones at that!"

Emily laughs.

"Okay then, King Brother Jimmy!

*****

"I just don't know what to think?" says Emily's mum, that evening, as they sit together on Emily's bed. The girl's mother came into her bedroom to find out the truth about her daughter's injured hand. One thing led to another. In tears, Emily opens up about Belinda, about the bullying and her suicidal thoughts. Her mum just listens, holding her daughter's hand, as it all pours out. The woman learns about 'an imaginary boy', though Emily says no more, and, for the first time in her life, discovers that her own mother, also teased as a child, had an imaginary friend called 'Jenny'. When told, in no uncertain terms, that imaginary friends are real, in their own dimension, and that because of this can travel via the eyes of someone else into their brains and witness relived memories, she asks her daughter to stop.

"Emily, I know you've had a hard time because of Belinda, and we all find ways of coping, but please... listen to me–"

"Mum! It's true! I just knew you wouldn't believe me. Think me crazy, like I was one of your patients. That's why I never told you before. But Granny knows. And this boy inside me was spot on about Lingling. She told me. But he and Jenny are so worried for Kami. Her brother coming into her bedroom when she's half-dressed and lying down with her on the bed. He says we just have to do something."

"This imaginary boy–?" begins Emily's mum.

"No, Kami's brother!" interrupts Emily, not wishing to discuss or involve Jimmy. "He's going to be priest, for God's sake!"

Exactly the same words used when Jimmy told her about what he saw going on in that bedroom.

"This girl you talk about. Did the imaginary boy inside you see anything happen to her?"

"Actually, he did."

"In the girl's bedroom?"

"Uh-huh!"

"Hmm! Look, ask your friends round to Granny's on Wednesday. That really will be nice, anyway. Not been to the Vale of Health for ages, myself, I've been that busy, but I'm really pleased you and Granny can share your music. But your dad and I are devastated about you injuring your hand. How could you have been so careless?"

Emily shrugs her shoulders. She's still not told her mother the truth about Belinda slamming the locker door on her hand. Didn't want to distract attention from poor Kami's plight.

"Accidents happen, Mum. It's why they're called accidents."

"No bones broken, thankfully. It'll get better. You and Lingling are sure to win this year. Granny's so proud of you."

Mother and daughter hug before Emily is left alone to make plans with her brother before drifting into a fretful sleep.

Chapter Eight

Not for a very long time has the little house in the Vale of Health seen so much activity. After a large plateful of the old lady's delicious muffins has been hungrily demolished, Lingling disappears into the music room with her friend's granny to fill the air with the divine music of Franz Schubert, whilst Emily, her mother and Kami sit on the sofa in the living room, together with Jimmy and Jenny who are both unseen but so very real for Emily.

Emily's mum puts her arm around Kami after telling the girl they know about her evil brother and what he does to her. Kami doesn't even ask how they know. She just sobs and sobs in Mrs Brownlie's arms whilst Jimmy and Jenny do some silent talking together, and, with Emily, across different dimensions.

"Do you think Kami's mum knows but doesn't dare say anything?" Jimmy asks.

"No!" replies his sister. "I know her. She wouldn't shy away from the truth. I'll tell you what, though. She'll kill Mark if she ever finds out."

"Can't have that," Jenny chips in. "Her mother arrested and put away for murder? Poor Kami! Better we get the brother where it'll really hurt. His so-called religion."

"Tell the Pope?"

"Not exactly. No, we need evidence. Then go to the

seminary. Show it to them."

"Emily... could you lend Kami your mobile?" asks Jimmy.

"You're joking!" Emily says aloud.

Her mother turns, sharply, to face her.

"Emily, what's got into you? Poor Kami here, then you come out with something like that!"

Emily had not been listening to her mother and her friend talking, quietly, about what the brother had got up to with his little sister over the years ever since she was at primary school.

"Sorry," she apologises to her re-found friend seated on the other side of her mother. "I was talking to myself. Like, after listening to things going on inside my head."

"Don't worry. My daughter's not mad, whatever those vindictive girls at your school are saying. I'm a doctor. I know about these things. A quarter or more children have imaginary friends who sometimes help them cope with life. And they're totally real for the child. Remember, Kami, not all big brothers are like Mark."

"I don't understand how you guys know so much. Or this imaginary person does."

"Kami, my dear girl, life itself is one big mystery. All I do know is that we doctors are here to help people like you. Now... let's hear what Emily has to say."

Emily gets up and goes to the other end of the couch to sit down next to Kami.

"How often does it happen, Mark coming into your

room, like, that when you're...?" She pauses, not sure what to say.

"When I'm half-naked? Whenever Mum and Dad are out together. Which is way too often. Mum's a hopeless cook, so they're always having meals out. And never ask me to join them. Big joke is that Mark was always supposed to be looking after me when I was little."

"And not abusing you!" adds Emily's mum.

"My *friend* (not wanting to call Jimmy 'brother' in front of her mother) says we need hard evidence and suggests I give you my mobile so that if it happens again, you can leave it turned on to record everything, unseen by your brother," says Emily.

Kami looks blankly ahead, without responding, as though turning the idea over in her head... over and over and over again.

"I've a better idea," chips in Emily's mum. "I have an old i-Phone that still works. Dad'll set it up for Kami, but in my name. If there's any legal come-back... and being a doctor I'm very suspicious of lawyers... then *I* can take the blame."

Emily frowns.

"Take the blame for trying to save Kami from her paedo big brother?"

"If necessary. Kami, is there somewhere in your bedroom you could hide it?"

Before the girl can answer, Jimmy tells Emily he knows the ideal spot.

"He's telling me something, Mum... wait a

moment..." She pauses, mouth open, as though listening attentively to words of wisdom from her brother who isn't there. "I've got it!"

"Well?" questions Emily's mum as she and Kami sit staring at Emily.

"The kangaroo's pouch!"

"He knows about Joey?" questions Kami, her eyes almost popping out in wonder at the mystery of the other girl's 'imaginary friend'.

"Joey the kangaroo?" grins Emily's mum. "I like it. A cuddly roo with a pouch?"

"My Aunty Jessie in Australia sent it to me when I was thirteen. She said every teenage girl needs a roo to look after her," declares Kami. "Fat lot of good it did me!"

"Do you think your aunt knew about Mark? Female intuition?" asks Emily.

"Dunno. But it's a good idea," agrees Kami. "Joey's usually sitting on the chair in the corner, facing my bed. A mobile phone would easily fit in his pouch and..."

"Wait, my imaginary friend's got another idea. Or rather, Jenny has. Granny's imaginary friend who's teamed up with him to help Kami."

Again, Emily sits opened mouthed for a few seconds, discoursing in her head with Jenny and Jimmy, before coming out with the invisible elderly teenager's suggestion: that Kami cut a small hole in Joey's pouch for the camera lens of the mobile. This way, Kami could make a full video recording of whatever takes place on her bed.

"And make sure the microphone isn't covered up," adds Emily after further instructions from Jimmy. Emily laughs. "Jenny just told my imaginary friend that she knows all about mobile phones now 'cos Granny's hopeless with tech stuff and she had to call on Jenny in her brain to help her with her own mobile when she first got one, a few years back, after Grandpa died."

As the Schubert Fantasy reaches a frenzied climax, just before that sudden pause before the hauntingly nostalgic return of the opening first subject, Emily, her mother and Kami sit spellbound, in silence, each wondering how, in a world that can produce music like that of the great Austrian composer, such awful things can happen to a young girl like Kami.

Already, Emily has forgotten about her injured hand which now seems of vanishing importance.

Chapter Nine

Emily's mother has to leave early to prepare a hurried meal for her dad, expected home any minute after a gruelling day in the operating theatre. Emily and her mum promise each other to make no mention of what took place in the Vale of Health for, whilst appearing to cope with anything and everything thrown at him in the hospital, privately the man struggles with family issues beyond the norm. If he were to find out the truth about how Emily got her hand injury, he would most certainly go straight round to Belinda's place to tear her and her family to shreds. As for Kami, he would, for sure, murder the brother on the road to becoming a priest.

Emily, Kami and Lingling stay on at Granny's for an evening meal together, consuming, with relish, what they find in the old lady's freezer. Beef hotpot, it turns out, plus, of course, another plateful of defrosted muffins. Bloated, they formulate plans together.

Hopefully, Emily's wrist will be sufficiently recovered to allow her to play the Schubert the following month, but, if not, Kami is abandoning her violin to learn the secondo part, with Lingling in primo in place of Emily. More importantly, Emily promises to get her mum's old i-Phone up and running for Kami before the weekend when, in all probability, Kami's parents will be going to the opera at Covent Garden. Their daughter heard talk about this and noticed her brother's eyes glint like red warning lights on mention of Don Giovanni. Kami swears she saw a glimpse of the Devil there. Emily reckons Mozart would have gone to town over a paedo priest like Mark, casting him into the flames of Hell against a surging backdrop in D minor like that Brahms piano concerto. Not Schubert's key of F minor. "No way in F minor," she tells a puzzled Kami and Lingling.

"Jenny's just come up with a suggestion," Granny says when the girls finally agree it's time for them to leave. Three heads turn to look, in eager anticipation, at the old Cockney woman.

"Ye-es?" asks Emily, slowly, half-expecting to hear a thought that has been forming in her own head. Was it Jimmy's thought? Often, she cannot be certain.

"Well, you're obviously like the three musketeers, now. Or 'musketresses'. One for all and all for one."

"Uh-huh!" Emily grunts, grinning, for she knows what Granny's about to say.

"So... Jenny thinks you should form a... now, what does she call it?"

"A club?" suggests the granddaughter.

"The very word that Jenny uses. A club to help troubled girls."

"Troubled girls?" questions Lingling.

"Like us. So, Jimmy and Jenny can help them like they're doing for us guys."

"And Jenny did for me years ago, a poor little bullied Cockney girl, ay?" chuckles Granny. "You could hold your meetings here. And just play on my Steinway if you run out of things to say."

"*Just* play the piano? Aren't you forgetting something, Granny?"

Emily, smiling, looks at her friends and winks.

"Muffins!" they shout out in unison.

"Muffins it is, then! And a name? For your club?" asks the old lady.

Emily looks sideways at Kami who nods in agreement.

"The Roo Club!" they announce together, thinking of Joey the soft toy kangaroo about to trap the evil brother.

Curiously, later that evening, as Emily crawls into bed nursing her injured hand, she's happier than she's ever felt since introducing the new girl, Belinda, to her music friends at school.

*****

The following Saturday morning, Kami spends time in her room with Emily's mum's refurbished i-Phone, cutting holes in Joey's pouch to accommodate the phone's camera lens, and microphone, without it being obvious, then placing the kangaroo in a position on her chair, phone in pouch, camera turned on, to ensure perfect recording of anything that might happen on her bed that evening.

Earlier, in the afternoon, the newly formed Roo Club meets in that little house in the Vale of Health, beside Hampstead Heath, to discuss how to take things forward. Emily's mum, with the authority of a doctor, has already spoken with the school's head teacher about her daughter's wish to form a club, at school, to help troubled girls. Mrs Gray thought it a splendid idea. So much so, she offered up her secretary's office, during lunch hour, once a week, on a Friday, when the secretary takes a half-day off, as the club venue. A notice about the 'Roo Club' is put up on the school notice board that first Thursday.

Friday, lunch time. The three founding members of the Roo Club sit, in respectful silence, in the school secretary's office adjacent to their headmistress's 'den', as they call it.

They start the very first meeting by establishing the tenets of their club. Emily, on Jimmy's suggestion, says they need three words to describe what they're about. Each girl has to come up with one suggestion.

"My choice," Emily informs the others, "is 'forgive'. I have to forgive my friends who abandoned me and made me feel suicidal."

"I was one of those, Em. I am so very sorry. And because you and your brother helped *me* so much, my word is 'help'," says Lingling.

"Up to me for the third word?" questions Kami.

"Uh-huh!" exclaimed Emily.

"My religion. It's supposed to be about *real* love. Not what Mark wanted to do to me. So, my word is... love."

"Good one, Kami. I'll let Mrs Gray know. She can put our tenets on the school poster."

But after forty minutes with not a single taker, Emily begins to have doubts about the idea to form a club to help others with problems. She stands up, about to suggest they call it a day, and that perhaps it isn't such a great idea anyway, when there's a timid knock on the door.

"Come in!" she calls out in as an authoritative voice she as can come up with.

The door opens and a girl in her class called Violet, once, but no longer, a good friend of Emily's, and who has become one of Belinda's most enthusiastic Emily-bullies, sheepishly enters. She looks at the three girls, shakes her head without saying a word, and is poised to leave the room when Emily says,

"Please, if you'd rather I'm not here, you can speak to Lingling and Kami on their own."

Violet, avoiding eye contact with her one-time friend, shakes her head again and remains by the door staring at her feet.

At first, Emily reckons Violet is only there to gather information to pass on to Belinda. "Just curious," was all she offers when asked why she came.

"We're here to help girls with *real* problems," says Lingling. "Like me with my dad being put in prison by the Chinese government for standing up for democracy in Hong Kong."

Violet merely shrugs her shoulders and looks quizzically from one to another of the three 'musketresses'.

"Now!" Jimmy suddenly announces, unheard in the real world, when Emily's tormentor looks directly into her eyes. In a flash, together with Jenny, Jimmy slips into the dark-haired girl's light brown eyes and zips back along an optic nerve, then on to a grim, noisy corner deep within her brain.

It's the shouting and yelling that lead Jimmy and his granny's imaginary friend to the girl's hippocampus where they immediately emerge in a kitchen, somewhere in Hampstead not far from the Vale of Health.

Violet was seated, leaning forwards with elbows on the kitchen table, her face in her hands and an untouched bowl of cereal in front of her.

"Stop it!" she screamed at her parents who, standing at opposite ends of the table, were hurling abuse, peppered with the 'f' word, at each other. Both stopped, momentarily, looked at Violet, then, as if the girl wasn't there, continued to bicker.

"Why?" the woman shouted. She walked round the table towards the man, went up close to him and poked him on the chest. "You ask why? I'll tell you, then. Because you're so bloody useless. That's why?"

"You f------ whore! I give you everything. Absolutely bloody everything! Pay for our daughter to go to a top London girl's school. Your idea. Then, on the sly, you decide to climb into bed with your randy boss."

"At least he's got what counts down there!" shouted the mother, at which Violet's father struck the woman so hard across the face with the back of his hand that her head twisted round.

"That's it! I'm off. Violet, pack your things. We're leaving. Now! I'll drop you off at school on the way to the university. And pick you up after work—"

"Oh no!" yelled Violet's father. "She stays here. You relinquished your right as a mother in that bastard's bed last night. 'Night out with the girls'? Not! Violet's mine now. *My* daughter! No longer yours."

"Sicko!" shouted the woman, rubbing her slapped face.

Violet scraped her chair away from the table, picked up the bowl of untouched cereal, and flung this over her squabbling parents, dousing them in milk and sugar puffs, before hurriedly leaving the kitchen, grabbing her school bag in the hallway, slipping on her blazer and leaving the house before slamming the front door behind her. Next thing, she was aware of her father standing and wiping sugar puffs off his shoulders and calling out to her from the gate, ordering her to come back straightaway, but, in tears, she merely hurried on up the hill towards Finchley Road tube station.

The vision vanishes. Jimmy and Jenny find themselves in silent darkness until, quite suddenly, they're walking in the school corridor with Violet clutching her school bag.

"There's Emily. Standing alone," whispers Jenny.

They see Emily smile in her usual, friendly way at Violet who looked away without acknowledging her, walking straight past Jimmy's sister to join Belinda and two other ex-friends of Emily: Sam, a budding clarinetist, plus a half-Russian girl, Ava, also a pianist.

Things go blurry. Misty. They're back in that kitchen with Violet sitting, alone, at the kitchen table, a half-eaten pizza in front of her.

The place was a mess with piles of unwashed plates and cups and cutlery littering the side board. The door was open, and a man's voice that Jimmy recognises as that of the girl's father, yelled abuse into a phone in the hallway beyond.

Chapter Ten

Jimmy, back with Emily who is now fully aware of why her one-time friend Violet has turned up at the Roo Club, sees his sister draw up a chair for the other girl.

"I don't feel like I'll ever be able to sing again," Violet tells Lingling.

Violet has the best singing voice in the school. When she sang solo in Mendelssohn's *'Oh For the Wings of a Dove'* at a public concert given by the school's best musicians, the local press said she had 'the voice of an angel'. How come she can no longer sing?

"Nonsense!" says Lingling. "Of course you can sing."

Violet bursts into tears. Lingling looks at Emily for help.

"It's like that Mendelssohn song, isn't it, Vi?" suggests Emily. "Trapped like a caged bird. Can't escape."

Violet nods without looking up.

"Your parents. Jimmy's told me what happened."

"What?" asks Kami. "Are they hurt? Oh, poor Vi..."

"No, *they've* hurt their only daughter, haven't they, Vi?"

Violet looks at Emily through her tears.

"How d'you know?"

"Because of my brother, Jimmy."

"But you haven't got a—"

"Yes, she has, Vi," interrupts Kami, "and he's really

65

helped Lingling and me. He's called Jimmy. And he's *inside* Emily."

"How can this Jimmy know about my parents?"

"By looking into your hippocampus," says Lingling.

"My what?"

"Hippocampus. Where you keep your memories."

Violet starts to get up, saying she thought the Roo Club really was for helping people with problems and not just a bunch of nutters, when Emily tells her sit down again.

"He saw you, in your hippocampus, sitting in your kitchen at home. Before you got up and threw a bowl of sugar puffs over your parents."

"Sugar puffs?" Kami covers a grin she cannot prevent. How she'd love to throw sugar puffs over her 'priestly' brother. No... a vindaloo curry would be better. "You've given me an idea, Vi," she says.

Emily looks crossly at Kami.

"This is serious!" she says. "Vi's parents were shouting and swearing at each other, because..." She reaches across with her uninjured hand to take Violet's hand. "Can I tell them, Vi? What Jimmy's just told me?"

Violet looks again into Emily's eyes.

"I'm so sorry," she says. "For being mean to you. It's just that..." she pauses.

"Just that tagging along with Belinda you felt free, like Mendelssohn's dove, right?"

"Right!" agrees Violet.

"What did Jimmy just tell you?" asks Lingling.

Violet gives consent for Emily to spill the beans by

nodding.

"Vi's mother had an affair with her boss at the university. Her parents rowed. Her dad hit her mum across the face. Her mum announced she was leaving. She wanted to take Vi, but her dad insisted she stay with him as her mum's the guilty party."

"And Jimmy knows this from my hippo... *hippo*thing?" queries Violet.

"Yes."

"And Jimmy's inside you? Like he's not even real?"

"Uh-huh!"

"Belinda says you're—"

"We're not here to talk about Belinda," chips in Kami. "That bitch can go jump for all I care. This is the Roo Club. Anyone with a problem like you have can join. To help others, too. Are you with us?"

Violet attempts a smile and nods.

"If your parents don't get back together again, who would you rather stay with?" Emily asks Violet.

The other girl responds immediately.

"Mum, of course."

Emily goes quiet whilst Jimmy talks to her.

"Jimmy says you witnessed your dad hit your mother really hard. He's violent, isn't he?" she says, passing on Jimmy's message for Violet's benefit.

"To Mum, yes. I think. Not to me. But I honestly don't blame her. I've never met this boss of hers, but he can't be worse than Dad. Hitting Mum like that. According to Mum, anyway, though it's the only time I've ever seen him hit her."

"Jimmy says your dad told you your mum's the guilty party and therefore you belong to him. Not true! By hitting your mum, *he* becomes the guilty party. At least that's what Jenny thinks."

"Jenny?"

"Granny's imaginary friend. Only with Granny being so old, she's become Jimmy's friend now. And *not* imaginary in their dimension. He and Jenny are always in each other's company, and Granny really doesn't mind."

"You should meet Emily's granny, Vi," insists Lingling. "Her muffins are awesome."

"Sunday?" suggests Emily "My granny's place, Vale of Health. We could go together, Vi."

*****

"Mum's got a call from Mr Hayes in Hong Kong," Lingling says, looking at her mobile phone after it pinged. "Wants me to phone her back."

She and Emily are walking to class together, discussing Violet's predicament, wondering how the Roo Club can help the girl. Lingling calls her mother, holds her phone to her ear and Emily can tell from the change in her friend's expression that the news is not good. As tears well in her eyes, Lingling talks quietly in Cantonese before putting her phone back in her bag.

"It's about Dad," she tells Emily. "He's been transferred to Mainland China."

"Oh my God, Lingling. I am so sorry!" Emily puts her uninjured arm around the other girl, just as Belinda, Sam and Ava appear from around the corner.

"Oooh! Take care, Lingling. You might catch something from her!" announces Ava, a heavily made-up blonde who proudly once told Lingling that she had a Chinese dragon tattooed below her belly button, now laughing and digging her elbow into Emily as the other two girls pass by.

"It's called syphilis," Belinda says without turning round. Emily reckons the girl hasn't actually looked her in the eye since her first day at their school before being introduced to Emily's friends. Now that Emily appears to have reclaimed two, maybe three, of those friends, her spite has turned even more venomous, and not once has she shown the slightest flicker of remorse for slamming Emily's hand in a locker door.

"Ignore her," says Lingling. "If only your brother Jimmy could help my dad. I can't bear to think what they'll do to him there in a Mainland prison."

"I'll have a word with Granny on Sunday. She gave a few concerts in China. Might have contacts. You never know."

"If only! So, you'll bring Vi on Sunday?"

"And we'll all find out whether Kami's saintly brother has been caught on camera with his trousers down? That was a brilliant idea, Emi," Jimmy whispers to his sister.

"Yeah," responds Emily. "And as for Kami's big brother, once Mum's got the bit between the teeth, there'll be no stopping her," replies Emily. "He won't know what's hit him."

Chapter Eleven

Emily and Violet meet up outside Golders Green tube station, after lunch, on Sunday, and take the number 210 bus to Jack Straws Castle before walking down the hill, together, towards the Vale of Health. As they enter the Vale, strains of piano music, barely audible at first, as if coming from another world, the beautiful but tortured world of Franz Schubert, lead them to the elderly pianist's home.

"Never knew Kami was that good on the piano," remarks Violet as they walk up the path towards the front door, four hands thumping out in fortissimo from the music room at the back.

"No! It's Granny playing secondo, Lingling at the top end. I can tell," Emily informs the other girl. "Something must be wrong."

"Wrong?"

"Kami *should* be playing. And yesterday, I wondered why she never messaged me. About that pervy, priestly prat of a brother of hers. And trapping him on Mum's old i-Phone. God, I hope she's okay. I'll never forgive Jimmy for coming up with the idea if..." Emily can't bear to think about the 'if'.

"Shall I ring the bell?" asks Violet.

"No! Got my own key."

Once inside, Emily hurries on ahead of Violet into the living room where Kami is seated on the settee, with Joey the kangaroo beside her, clutching the refurbished i-Phone. She hands this to Emily without saying anything. The phone's screen is shattered.

"Did Mark do this?" asks Emily.

Kami nods, looks up at Emily, and Jimmy seizes the chance. He grabs Jenny's hand, and in no time, together, they find themselves, once again, in Kami's hippocampus...

*****

Immediately, they see Kami, fully clothed, lying on her bed, her violin beside her. The bedroom door opens and...

The girl's brother entered, like before, trouserless. Jenny gasps for he wasn't even wearing underpants. In his hand was what appeared to be an item of female underwear.

He held this up for Kami to see.

"Knickers for Knickers!" he announced with pride, grinning. "Put them on. Now!"

Kami tried not to look as her brother, naked from the waist down, approached her bed. He threw a pair of filmy, white, silk panties down onto the bed beside her.

"Need to know whether they fit you. Bought them in your name, see. Using Dad's credit card. So, you have been a naughty little girl spending his money on pretty underwear, haven't you? Oh... *and* I bought this. I mean, *you* bought it."

Mark opened his hand to reveal a gold cross on a chain.

"Twenty-two carat gold. Won't say how much it cost Dad. But I'll not tell if you behave like a good little girl.

Here and now. The cross can remind you about God. Through our Lord, Jesus Christ."

He pointed to the silk panties on the bed.

"'Put them on,' I said. Straightaway! For God."

Slowly, Kami got up off the bed, turned around, slipped down her skirt, then her knickers, before putting on the silk underwear purchased by her brother with their father's money. Visibly trembling, she lay back on the bed, stiff and still and staring up at the ceiling. Her brother, shameless in his below-the-waist nudity, climbed up onto the bed beside her before placing a hand on her belly over the newly purchased silken underwear.

"Remember, Knickers, our bodies belong to our Lord. We are merely their caretakers. Will you not please the Lord and show him how much...?"

Mark paused, then patted his sister's hand that she held in a tight fist. For a glorious moment, Jimmy imagined the girl punching her brother in the face, but, instead, the brute uncurled her fingers, lifted her limp hand up and onto his own belly.

"We have to do something," whispers Jimmy. "We must help her."

"Can't," responds Jenny. "Remember? This is what happened. Yesterday. But look at Joey. His pouch is facing the bed like Kami said it would at the Roo Club meeting. I just pray that..."

Jenny pauses as the other girl's brother continued his hideous soliloquy:

"...How much you appreciate his creations. Which,

of course, includes your elder brother. You may touch it."

It?

"Jesus!" exclaims Jimmy, unheard by the two central characters in that horror movie playing in Kami's hippocampus.

Quite suddenly, Kami sprang upright, screaming. She tore herself away from Mark when he attempted to pull her back down. She scrambled from the bed, reached down for her strewn clothes and held these up in front of her.

"Go away! This is so bloody wrong. You know it. I know it. Nothing to do with God. Get out of my room or I'll call the police."

"'Bloody' ay? Such language! Ooh, you bad, bad girl! Now, calm down, Knickers—"

"And don't you dare call me 'Knickers' again. You're a psycho. I'm going next door. To the neighbours' place. Right now!"

"Oh, you are *such* a naughty little girl. I really will have to teach you a..."

Kami ran to the chair, picked up Joey the kangaroo, but before she could reach the door, Mark was off the bed and blocking her way. He whisked the soft toy animal out of his sister's hands.

"Oh my God, he's gonna find the mobile phone," gasps Jimmy. But he isn't sure whether to gasp in horror or breathe a sigh of relief over what followed...

Holding the kangaroo, the budding priest strode over to the window, opened it and threw the little Ozzie soft toy animal out of the girl's bedroom.

"You're far too old to play with dolls and stuff. As for our neighbours, they hate the noise you make with that thing!" He pointed to Kami's beloved violin on the floor beside her bed. "Perhaps it should go the same way as that annoying little kangaroo if..."

Mark paused and stared, like a predatory snake, at his sister as if working out the best course of action under the circumstances.

"If... and *only* if... you continue to be a naughty girl. I'm prepared to let you off lightly, this time, if you behave. Plus, I'm tired. Been studying St Paul's Epistles all afternoon. You could learn something from him. Faith, Hope and Love, right? Love for your elder brother? All right, I'll go back to continue my study if you promise to behave. And next time, please show some respect for God's beloved creations."

The would-be priest looked meaningfully down at a part of his anatomy that should either be covered up or... or, in Marks case, removed for good, Jimmy reckons.

Kami nodded, without saying anything, and Jimmy seethes as he watches the trouserless trainee priest leave the girl's bedroom.

"The absolute bastard!" he says to Jenny. "Plus, he's gone and destroyed the evidence."

Darkness, like a curtain coming down. Then the imaginary brother and imaginary friend, in shock and still together inside Kami's hippocampus, are outside the same house in North London watching the girl, now fully clothed, search the flowerbeds till she picked up Joey the kangaroo and removed the i-Phone. They can see its screen is fractured. When the girl tried to turn the thing on and open the apps, nothing happened. They see her burst into tears, then everything goes blank.

Muffled sobs seeping into the darkness almost tear Jimmy's heart out, if, indeed, imaginary beings do have hearts. Jimmy vows to ask Emily when they return to her world, though he doubts she'll have an answer for him. Both brother and sister have been puzzled and uncertain about the different realities of their separate states of existence ever since they first became aware that each had sibling in another dimension.

Chapter Thirteen

The music stops. Moments later, Lingling appears in the doorway.

"I heard the front door opening. Kami's far too upset to play the Schubert with me, so your lovely granny has been down in the lower register. She is so awesome, Emily. Why did you say she can no longer play?"

"Not like she used to, Lingling. But you sounded pretty amazing up there in the primo part. We might even swap round for the Festival Competition if..." Emily holds up her injured hand.

"You'll get better. You must! So..." she begins, turning to look at Kami who still holds up the broken i-Phone for all to examine, "the phone your mum gave Kami. Can we get anything from it? It looks terminally dead to me. Thrown out of a first-floor window by that bully of a brother of hers, Kami said."

"I know. Jimmy told me. He saw it all happen. With Jenny. In Kami's hippocampus. If only we could get that footage, we'll have the little shit by the balls."

"If he has any!"

Emily laughs, at which moment her granny hobbles into the sitting room.

"Has any what?" the old lady asks.

"Balls. Kami's paedo brother."

"Mmm! Whatever! That broken phone your mother gave her. I'm afraid I belong to the wrong century to know anything about fixing those horrid things. What about your dad?"

"Not interested if he can't cut into it with a scalpel," replies Emily.

"Sam's dad might help."

All eyes turn towards Violet who speaks for the first time since entering the little house in the Vale of Health.

"Sam's dad?" questions Emily. "Why? How?"

"Well, apparently he's always on at her about how amazing her baby sister is, apparently, but never gives her credit for anything. He works as an IT consultant for a finance company in the City. If anyone knows how to fix a broken i-Phone, or at least retrieve data recorded on it, he's your man. Maybe if Sam shows some interest in his line of work by asking him to fix it, he might appreciate *her* a bit more."

"You're right," agrees Emily. "Before Belinda—"

"Hey, that's a good one!" interrupts Lingling. "B.B. Before Belinda. As in B.C.... Before Christ."

"Na! She's not that important. Where was I? So... if Sam shows an interest in her dad's computer stuff, like i-Phones and that, then he might appreciate his elder daughter's clarinet playing. Remember how well she played the slow movement of the Mozart Clarinet Concerto last year? And he wasn't even there at the concert."

"Yeah! Sam was livid. He stayed at home to play with her little sister rather than coming to hear her perform. Her mum was furious."

"I could ask her," suggests Violet. "At the worst, she'll only say, 'No!'"

Kami hands the phone to Violet.

"All sorted then?" asks Granny. "So, how's about a muffin or two?"

"Or three or four?" adds Emily.

"A whole plateful would be nice," offers Lingling, laughing.

When Granny disappears off into the kitchen, Emily asks the Chinese girl how come she's so cheerful after what her mother told her about her father.

"We had a long chat before attacking Schubert," says Lingling.

"Poor Schubert!"

"No, your granny is so incredible. She even has contacts in China. Like high up, important people. Plus, she donated money to a music school in Beijing. There's this guy high up in the Communist Party who will listen to her. She's sure of it."

"Hey, I've an idea," suggests Emily.

"I like your ideas. Tell me!"

"Granny could be our official Roo Club advisor. Maybe even come to the school on Fridays. Might attract more customers." She looks across at Violet who is busily comforting Kami. "Bet there are dozens out there who could do with our help"

"And Jimmy's and Jenny's," adds Lingling. "By the way, Vi. Did you know Sam's mother's poorly with rheumatoid arthritis, and things have become a thousand times worse? Sam's irritating little sister is forever telling lies to their dad about Sam who can no longer get support from their mum, and their dad's at his wit's end trying to hold things together."

"Too busy to fix the phone, then?"

"No! The opposite. He'd be doing what he loves the most. Like fiddling with a broken phone. Trying to retrieve lost data, perhaps. It'll help to bond them."

"Good Roo Club business, then?"

"Yeah! Good business!" Lingling holds up her right hand to high five with Emily's good hand.

*****

"Sam, we need to talk," Violet says, leaving a message on Sam's phone that evening. "Please. It's important. Could save someone's life."

She hesitates before adding the last sentence, wondering whether it was overly melodramatic, but decides to leave it in. After all, if *she* had been molested like poor Kami, she'd certainly feel suicidal.

Her dad knocks on her bedroom door.

God, is he going to turn into a priest and molest me now Mum's gone?

"What d'you want?" she calls out, grumpily.

"Just... just want to talk, Vi. Apologise."

Apologise? God Almighty!

"Go away!"

There's a thud, then a peculiar growly noise that Violet cannot make out until she realises her father is crying out there on the landing. She opens the door to find him slumped like a beached whale up against the wall, sobbing. The anger, smouldering inside her since

79

that fateful breakfast, vanishes. She kneels down and puts her arm around him, just as he used to do with her whenever she hurt herself as a small child.

"I'll make you a cup of tea, Dad. And we can talk. Okay?"

She helps him up and leads him, by the hand, a grown man turned child, downstairs. She sits him down at the kitchen table where it all happened that fateful sugar puff morning, puts the kettle on, then joins him.

"Wish I had one of Emily's granny's muffins to give you," she says. It's all she can think of saying as, all of a sudden, her mind seems to be turned upside down.

"The police came round," her father tells his daughter. "At the office. Everyone staring at me. They took me..." He pauses and holds his head in his hands.

"What? The police?" Violet hasn't a clue what her father's talking about.

"Mum. She called the domestic abuse squad or whatever. Couple of police officers turned up at work, took me into a separate room and grilled me for half an hour like I was a criminal. Showed me a photo Mum took of her reddened cheek where I hit her. I kept saying I didn't mean it, and that's true. Just lost all self-control. That's all. Nothing criminal, I promised them. But they weren't interested in my excuses. Didn't seem to be listening when I told them about her affair. Getting pushed over the brink when she taunted me with being 'Useless down there'."

"Dad... I'm so sorry I threw sugar puffs all over you guys."

Violet's father laughs and cries at the same time.

"It was what we both needed. Look, it's you I must apologise to, Violet. I just saw red. Couldn't stop myself. Completely lost control, and it was as if..." He pauses and looks at his daughter who takes hold of his hand and gives it a squeeze. She, too, is now in tears.

"...As if *you* weren't there," continues Violet's father.

"Dad, I'm here to listen, okay? Not judge."

"Impotence."

"You?"

"Going on a couple of years. Caused a big rift between Mum and me. No, that's an understatement. Bloody Grand Canyon. Excuse the French."

Violet wants to laugh but can't.

"Mum just made me feel useless. Redundant. Kept on saying things like, 'If I was a proper man...'. I knew she needed it. The sex. It's the way she's always been, and when we had you it was..." He pauses. "It was glorious. And you appeared. We were so happy back then."

"Did you see the doctor, Dad? Surely there are pills that could help you."

"Been there. Done that."

"Counselling."

"Mum wouldn't have it. I knew there was something going on between her and that bugger of a boss of hers but didn't dare confront her. Until..."

"Yes?"

"I happened to bump into one of the ladies she was

supposed to be having a night out with. She knew. Like it was some kind of a joke. Couldn't hide it from me when I asked why she wasn't with Mum and those other so-called friends she was supposed to have been with that evening. It all came out and I felt such an idiot. I think the woman actually enjoyed telling me. Like it was all my fault. That really drove it in."

"Tea, Dad?"

Violet's father nods.

As Violet makes her father a cup of tea, he tells her how the police cautioned him, and told him he would be hearing from her mum's solicitor. Apparently, they showed no interest in his motive for lashing out that morning. Not their problem.

Later, after Violet has returned to her room, she feels confused. Her mum's good fun and they always have great times together. But her dad's the sensitive one. When she was little, *he* was the one who always comforted her and who told her bedtime stories. The only person she truly wanted to hate was her mother's boss. Taking advantage. Using her as a sex object and destroying their lives. Then allowing lawyers, who knew nothing about her, decide her fate. *He* was the one Violet should have showered with sugar puffs that morning!

Chapter Fourteen

A message from Sam...

'I'm the one whose life needs saving. They're driving me mad! Your place in half an hour.'

Violet wasn't sure, her dad being in such a state. There again, it might do him good to meet one of his friends. Sam, too, had parental problems. Her mum sick, her dad all over Sam's little sister. She might be understanding.

The doorbell rings. Violet's dad opens the door before she manages to get downstairs.

"A friend of yours, Vi," he calls out as she's on her way down. "Sam!" The girl in the doorway offers a friendly smile enough to melt the heart of anyone so frozen in despair, like Violet's father, that he can hardly take in another breath.

"Come in," Violet says, over her father's shoulder. "Sorry, Dad. Should've said I've invited Sam round."

"Lovely to meet you, Sam," her father welcomes the girl. "Please come in. I'll make another cup of tea, ay, Vi?"

"Erm... I don't think Sam's *really* into tea, Dad."

"G & T?"

"She's fifteen! Like me. We'll be in my room if you need me."

The two girls leave Violet's father standing alone in the hallway as they go on up the stairs.

"Your dad seems so nice," Sam says once inside

Violet's bedroom. "Wish I could say the same about mine."

"Actually, it's *your* dad I want to talk to you about."

"*My* dad? Unless it involves that annoying baby sister of mine, he'll not be interested. God, I hate him!"

"Sam?"

"Ugh! She's taken to telling tales about me. Mum used to keep her under control, but since her illness, rheumatoid arthritis, it's called, Sarah's had him twisted round her little finger. 'Dad... Sam, won't let me strangle her! You will say 'Yes', won't you?'"

Violet laughs.

"I nearly strangled both *my* parents the other morning. They had a flaming row whilst I was having my sugar puffs. Only these ended up all over them. With the milk."

"You flung your sugar puffs over your parents?" Sam looks shocked. She sits down on the bed and Violet sits beside her.

"I totally lost it, Sam," continues Violet. "Anyway, you don't want to hear about *my* troubles. And I am so sorry to hear about that beastly little brat of a sister of yours. But what I have to say might just help you bridge the gap between you and your dad."

"How?"

"Well... he's into IT, right? Computers and stuff?"

"It is his job. He's teaching Sarah all about the one he's just given her and she's only bloody nine years old."

"Here's your bridge, then. Kami's brother has been abusing her."

Sam goes silent for a few moments before turning to look Violet in the eye.

"What did you just say?" she asks.

"Sam's brother..."

"The priest?"

"Trainee, or whatever. He's a paedo. Like really, really pervy. Does it..." She pauses.

"Does what?"

"Abuses her. Or tries to. When their parents aren't at home, and *he's* supposed to be looking after his little sister."

"He could give Sarah a run for her money for all I care," announces Sam.

"Sam, this is dead serious. Like I messaged you. He... that is *Emily's* brother..." Violet has obvious difficulty saying what she's wanting to say.

"Your Roo Club stuff? You should hear what Belinda has to say about all that nonsense."

"It's *not* nonsense, Sam. Honest. You've no idea how helpful Emily and her brother have been to some of us."

"Emily's got a brother? News to me!"

"I'll get round to that. The point is, we, Emily included, set a trap for the perv. She gave Kami an old i-Phone they got refurbished and hid it in Kami's kangaroo's pouch..."

Sam chuckles.

"The Roo you named the club after?"

"Yeah! *That* kangaroo. And we were gonna record what goes on in Kami's bedroom. When their parents went to the opera. And as we predicted–"

"We? The Roo Club?"

"With Emily's mum and her amazing Granny. Plus Jimmy, her big brother. I'll tell you about them later. As I was saying, Mark, Kami's brother, came into her bedroom with nothing on below the waist—"

"Are they nudists or something?"

"Please let me explain, Sam. That brother of hers went into her room, half naked, tells her to put on a pair of frilly knickers he just bought for her with their dad's credit card and wants her to touch him... there!"

"What!?" Sam's expression changes from one of mild amusement to horror. "No way! Surely not?"

"Surely, yes... poor Kami! She's had to cope with the bastard for years, only it's suddenly gotten a whole lot worse. Now she's older, like. Reckons he can get away with anything 'cos he's a seminarian. Thing is, their dad thinks the sun shines out of the brother's saintly arse. So proud to be having a priest in the family, he tells everyone. Anyway, poor Kami was absolutely terrified. She screamed at him to get out of her room, and he grabbed the kangaroo... it's called Joey–"

"Joey?" queried Sam.

"Yeah, Joey... And he threw it out the window, mobile phone and all."

"And the phone's broken and you want to know whether Dad can fix it?"

"Or at least retrieve the recording of what Mark did and said."

"Vi, I'll do anything to catch a shit like that. But my

dad?"

"Surely he can help us?"

"When all he does is go on about me being mean to his darling little Sarah? Fat chance!"

"Will you at least *meet* with Kami? And the rest of us?"

"And Emily's brother?"

Violet goes silent, then smiles to herself, unseen by Sam.

"Jimmy? Maybe!" she says temptingly.

Suddenly, Sam seems interested. "When? Where? If Belinda sees me anywhere near Emily, she'll go ballistic. Tear my eyes out, for sure. Promise you won't tell?"

"What's Emily ever done to make Belinda be so mean to her? I went along with Belinda at first 'cos... well, Emi *is* different. Strange, you could say. Talks funny. And to herself, at times. But she'll do anything to help others."

"Yeah! That's why Belinda calls her 'Miss Goody Two Shoes' after that announcement by Mrs Gray at school assembly about the Roo Club."

"And Kami? Will *you* at least help us to help *her*? Save her life, perhaps, like I said."

"I'll think about it," comes the reply.

*****

Sam does. Think about it, that is. And Violet's dad thinks about her. Sam. Or rather, her smile. He has forgotten how pleasant it is to be smiled at by any female. And without telling his daughter, he goes onto an online dating agency. But that, dear reader, is a whole different story.

Sam agrees to join the 'Roo Crowd', as Belinda scornfully calls Emily, Lingling and Kami, in that little house in the Vale of Health, on Wednesday afternoon. Like the others, she has concocted a plausible, but untrue, reason for absconding from sport. None of the music students are particularly sporty, anyway. Nor is their head teacher, Mrs Gray... also a musician.

Before Wednesday, Jimmy has an opportunity to learn, via Emily, from Violet, about the meeting with Sam. Or rather, from the other girl's hippocampus to which, without knowing, he has always had instant access through his sister's eyes. Desperate to save Kami with the gorgeous blue eyes from the unwanted attentions of her not-so-saintly seminarian brother, he talks things over with Jenny who, by his reckoning, is as wise as she is beautiful. Her solution puzzles him, but he has to bow to her seventy-plus years of experience...

"Tell Sam to bring her bring her little sister with her for a *special* treat. Muffins! If she can get Sarah on her side, then their dad might well agree to have a look at the broken i-Phone."

"Jenny, I'd never even have thought of that."

"Because you don't think like a girl. It's got a name, our sought of reasoning."

"Hmm! 'Fizzpopping'?"

Jenny gives Emily's brother a playful punch in the side.

"Lateral thinking, you numpty! We girls use it all

the time without even meaning to."

"Okay, then. I'll tell Emily to suggest it. Meanwhile, *we* have to think of a way to stop Kami's parents going out again till we've seen that video footage."

"No, we don't. Kami comes for a sleepover with you guys if they're planning an evening out together. No probs. I just know that Emily will agree. Lateral thinking again, Jimmy!"

Chapter Fifteen

Emily agrees with Jenny's lateral thinking and has no doubts that Granny will win over Sam's recalcitrant little sister and, through her, Sam's IT-savvy dad. More determined than ever to save Kami from the 'Demon Priest' as Jimmy now calls the girl's elder brother, she goes to bed feeling strangely happy.

"Thank you, Brother," she whispers before drifting off to sleep.

*****

"Emily?"

"Lingling? What are you doing calling me at this hour? It's bloody 2 am!"

Emily, clutching her phone to her ear, roles sleepily onto her back and stares at the empty darkness above her bed. Somehow, it reminds her of those black holes Jimmy goes on about. He gets quite excited about them. And about other science stuff. He's forever telling Emily how scientists are 'probing the nature of reality' as he likes to put it. Whenever she asks him 'what with?' he goes silent and shrugs a pair of shoulders that no none else can see.

"Not in China, it isn't. It's 10 o'clock there," explains Lingling. "And I'm so excited. Mr Hayes just got in touch with Mum, and she's texted me about it. Wants me to call him back in Hong Kong. My English is better than Mum's, and his Cantonese is rubbish." Lingling giggles. "The way he pronounces some of the Chinese words can make them sound really rude." Lingling pauses, then... "I wanted Jimmy to know, and we may need his help."

"You'd have to make a video call for him to see into your eyes. And we've never done that hippo thing over the phone before. It may not work. Why d'you need to be in touch with Jimmy through me, anyway?" Emily asks.

"Find out what to do next. About my dad. But I'm scared. What if it's *bad* news? Mum used the word 'progress'. Because of that guy your granny contacted. She thought that was a good word but wants me to find out."

"Why don't you just phone Hong Kong right now?"

"I want you to be with me. Jimmy, too."

"There's that little café near Finchley Road station. Along the Finchley Road towards Golders Green."

"I know it."

"See you there 7.15. For breakfast. It'll be midafternoon for Hongkongers. I know the café opens really early on weekdays. Dad's used it on occasions when on call for the hospital. Now get some sleep!"

"Good news, huh?" whispers Jimmy before Emily disappears into dreamland. "'Progress' can only mean one thing. Good old Granny, ay?"

*****

Lingling is there already, by herself, with a glass of milk and an untouched bacon toastie. She doesn't appear to notice Emily enter the café as she sits staring at the toastie as though wondering whether it's about to leap

91

up off the plate and bite her on her little Chinese nose. Jimmy loves her nose. In fact, he loves everything about the girl and hasn't stopped praying all night, inside his sister's head, that 'progress' really is good news.

Lingling almost jumps out of her school uniform in alarm when Emily taps her on the shoulder.

"Thank you so much," says Lingling. "Poor Mum hasn't slept all night."

She looks up at Emily, and Jimmy and Jenny slip quietly into her hippocampus...

******

Somewhere in there, Lingling is a small child, no more than five years old by Jimmy's reckoning. A memory...

She was being carried on her father's shoulders, bouncing up and down with excitement as they wound their way along a narrow street heaving with happy folk. There were brightly lit, colourful paper lanterns everywhere. In shop windows, dangling from poles and dancing from the hands of grinning Chinese guys hopping and skipping about in rhythm to the playful tunes of an *erhu*.

"When will we see the dragon, Baba?" the child asked in English.

"Soon," her father replied. "First, we take the MTR to Ocean Park. There you can see your dragon."

Flash forwards, and Lingling, now standing beside her father, her small hand held safely in his firm but gentle grip, was watching the dragon, open-mouthed and in awe, as it stepped forwards and backwards, this way and that, its huge mouth flapping and its friendly eyes seeking her out as it danced in time with the beats of the drums and the clashes of the cymbals. There were lanterns everywhere. Even floating high in the sky. When the dragon came up close, Lingling, a little scared, put her small arms around her father's legs, so strong and so safe; scared even after he reassured her that the dragon was good, and that he wanted to tell her that her ancestors, now with the Jade Emperor, will always look after her.

Moments later, Jimmy is back with Emily and Lingling in that little café on the Finchley Road, having left Jenny behind in Hong Kong and inside Lingling, because, as she told him, she was 'having the time of her life watching the dragon dance at the lantern festival!'. But Jimmy knows Emily might need him should 'progress' be in the wrong direction.

"Ready?" Emily asks Lingling. The Chinese girl looks up at her friend, and Jimmy has great difficulty in deciding whether he prefers her chocolate brown eyes to Kami's sky-blue ones.

Lingling taps her phone. Moments later, she gasps, for there, on the screen is the wonderful, grinning face of her father.

"Baba!" she shrieks.

There is sudden silence in the little café as everyone turns to look at the Chinese girl staring at the screen of her mobile phone. One scruffy looking fellow in a shabby worker's overall gets up, comes over to their table and peers over Lingling's shoulder at the smiling Chinese face on the screen. He grins and waves at the face. Lingling's father waves back.

"Good morning!" he says. "*Chī le ma?*"

"What's he saying?" the workman asks Lingling.

"He says, 'Have you eaten?' It's a polite form of greeting in Mandarin."

"Oh!" says the man. He gives Lingling's father a thumbs up. "Egg, sausage and baked beans plus a cuppa."

"Baba, what's happening?" the girl asks.

"I'm coming to London, Lingling. Earliest possible flight. Is Mama with you?"

"No. I'm with a friend. On my way to school. I'll tell her to call you."

"Wait!" insists Emily. She pulls out her own mobile, turns it on and gives it to Lingling. "Call her on my phone. She can see and talk with him on yours."

"That's what Jenny calls feminine lateral thinking!" Jimmy informs his sister.

Soon, Lingling's father and mother, thousands of miles apart, are talking excitedly to each other, in Cantonese, into mobile phones. The scruffy workman is now joined by several other customers and staff in that little café, none understanding a single word of the conversation.

"Why are they both crying," a woman asks.

Emily explains why whilst Lingling joins in the Chinese conversation.

"Her Dad's just been released from prison in China," Emily says. "Because of my granny."

"Your grandmother here put the girl's father in

prison in China?" a man asks.

Emily laughs.

"Not exactly!" she says. "Lingling's father was imprisoned for protesting about the changes in Hong Kong introduced by the Mainland Communist Party. They put their dummies in control and Hongkongers' independence got threatened. My granny has connections on the Mainland. Through her music. And..." She points to the happy tearful face of Mr Tan on the screen of Lingling's mobile. "He's a free man now!"

"Her dad's free!" announces the proprietor. "You know what this means, everyone!"

All turn to look at him.

"Free tea all round! Come and fill up your mugs, ladies and gents!"

Chapter Sixteen

"**I** need to tell you something, Sis."

"I'm really busy, Jimmy. In the middle of a maths lesson," Emily says inside her head. "What is it?"

"I've decided to become a writer!"

"A writer!?" the girl exclaims aloud.

Heads turn, including that of Belinda. She nudges the elbow of the half-Russian girl, Ava, seated next to her, and, looking meaningfully back at Emily, whispers in the other girl's ear. Ava chuckles. Thankfully, the maths teacher takes no notice, The lesson continues, and, inside her head, which has little space for maths anyway, Emily asks her brother what on earth put such crazy idea into his imaginary head.

"All these stories," replies Jimmy. "Lingling's, Kami's, Violet's and now Sam's. They've gotta be written down. I know you're far too busy, so whilst you're having fun with maths and stuff, I could get down to serious writing."

"In your dreams," Emily mutters aloud, to herself. More giggles from Belinda and Ava in front of her. Emily has known for a long time that her unusual behaviour, which includes appearing to talk to herself when, in fact, she's having a very real (real?) conversation with Jimmy, has given those girls a good excuse to bully and tease her, but it's hardly her fault that *she* was given a brother who resides inside her rather than outside, in flesh and blood, visible and audible to all and sundry.

Later, whilst pondering over a boringly difficult maths problem, she thinks that maybe Jimmy is right. Perhaps the activities of the Roo Club do need to be recorded for posterity, although the way Jimmy, now bursting with testosterone, goes on about Lingling's little nose and Kami's gorgeous blue eyes, means her brother may not be the right person for the job. Probably something to discuss at the next Friday Roo Club meeting, she reckons, before returning to a terrifying page of numbers and mathematical symbols.

*****

Mid-morning break, and Lingling is virtually bouncing up and down with excitement. Her Baba is arriving, by plane, early Saturday morning and wants to go straight to Emily's Granny's place to thank the old woman who, in all probability, has saved his life. Jimmy can hardly wait to meet the man, although Emily prays that this isn't to ask permission to one day marry his daughter.

"She'd never be able to see you!" Emily reminds him. "And you'd not see her without me being around. Not much of a life for either of us!"

"I do wish Jenny would stop going on about being seventy-seven," is Jimmy's response.

"So this is really about you and Jenny, right?"

"Best friend I've ever had," he replies. "Apart, of course, from my little sister. So... Sam's agreed to bring *her* baby sister, Sarah–"

"Jimmy, I am *not* a baby!" interrupts Emily.

"As I was saying, bring her little sister to the Vale of

Health on Wednesday. Have you told Granny to make extra fresh muffins, or should I ask Jenny to do that?"

"Me. Have to call her about Mr Tan coming on Saturday, anyway. D'you think he'll like muffins too? Do they have them in China?"

"Don't know anything about the Chinese and muffins. Only that Chinese girls have little noses. Which kind of suit girls. I think."

"Shut up!"

Which Jimmy happily does whilst listening to, and watching, the Chinese girl through Emily's eyes, as she talks to his sister about Hong Kong as it used to be before the Communist crackdown pre-COVID. He wishes he could tell Lingling that he saw her, as a little child, on her father's shoulders, on her way to watch the dragon dance in Ocean Park during the Lantern Festival, but sadly their separate realities prevents him from doing so.

*****

Emily and Jimmy are surprised to find Sam and Sarah already at Granny's place when they arrive there on Wednesday afternoon. Surprised, too, to discover that Sarah is a perfectly normal little girl, with the very same blue eyes as her big sister, and not a ghoulish monster with massive canine teeth and large claws to match. Just a little girl, clutching a raggedy doll called, of all things, Claribel.

"How did she come up with a name like that," Jimmy asks, in silence, of his sister. Emily questions the child on his behalf, and is told, in no uncertain terms, that it was the name of her friend who no one else could see, so she turned her into the doll that her mummy had as a child to make her come real.

"Do you talk to her?" asks Emily, glancing at Sam for a response. The big sister merely shrugs her shoulders.

"Of course I do," says Sarah as though the answer is so obvious it was hardly worth Emily asking the question.

"Well, shall I let you into a little secret?"

The younger girl grins, then nods her head. She comes up close to Emily.

"My Granny has had a friend all her life that no one else can see or hear. Do you want to know her name?"

Sarah nods again, shyly.

"She's called Jenny."

After a short pause, during which the child is clearly turning things over in her head, she gets up and runs off into the kitchen to find Emily's granny and introduce Claribel to Jenny. Moments later, she comes skipping back into the room, followed by Granny, to approach Violet, sitting by herself, with an untouched muffin on a plate on her lap. Sarah holds Claribel up in front of the older girl.

"Claribel wants to know why you're looking so sad," the child announces. She turns to look at Emily's granny. "And so does Jenny, doesn't she?"

Granny sits down next to Violet.

"It's the untouched muffin, Violet. Can mean only one thing," the old lady says. Violet just stares at the muffin as if trying to work out what it really is. Something edible or something that could destroy her? "Emily told me about your parents."

"Claribel wants to know why your parents are making you sad," says Sarah before climbing onto Violet's lap and handing the doll to the older girl. "She thinks parents should only make you happy."

Through Emily's eyes, Jimmy listens and watches as Violet offers titbits about her parents' fractured relationship to the child seated on her lap. A little girl who mops up every word with big wide eyes until...

Violet looks at Emily and Jimmy seizes the chance, taking Jenny with him. Once again, they find themselves in the young singer's hippocampus, now sitting in a café, near the girls' school, with her mother...

*****

"Dad says it's the only time he's ever hit you. Says you were goading him and that he's been struggling with..." Violet paused. "With his sex problem."

"Impotence," whispers Jimmy to Jenny. "It's called impotence, you know."

"I keep telling you, I have been around for seventy-seven years. I do know what impotence is, but can't see why it should be a problem. Not if they love each other."

"I think I love Violet, now. I mean, she does have lovely hair, doesn't she!? But what about Kami's eyes and Lingling's nose?"

"Oh, do stop going on about those poor girls and listen to what Violet's mum has to say in her defence. The girl's dad has a point. His wife broke her marriage

100

vows. She *is* the guilty party."

Violet's mother took a sip from her cup, as if buying time before she could come up with a truthful answer to her daughter's question.

"It's not that simple," she finally said.

"Yes, it is, Mum! You told me it wasn't the first time Dad hit you. And when the police came round with that photo of you with a red cheek and cautioned him, it seemed like he was some kind of monster."

"And no doubt he's saying the same about me. A bitch of a wife who has it off with her randy boss, ay?"

"Mum, I only want to know the truth. I'm being pulled apart here. Do I have any say in what happens to me, or will it be it up to the lawyers to decide?"

"Whatever happens, Vi, you must know that I love you."

"That's what Dad says, too."

"We both want the best for you."

"The best? Cut me in half, then. You take the left half and Dad has the right half!"

Violet's mother reached out to take her daughter's hand, but the girl pulled her hand away.

"Why can't you answer my question? Did he or did he not hit you before that morning when I threw my sugar puffs over you two. I really *had* had enough."

"Not exactly. But were times when–"

"So, Dad's telling the truth! He never hit you before and when he found out about you and your boss he just lost control."

"You make it sound so... so—"

"So what? So simple? You had an affair because Dad was impotent, and you needed a..." Violet got up abruptly. "Dad's right. You just wanted to be fucked!" the girl yelled. Heads turned to look at the mother and daughter. "And don't go blaming your randy boss. You were on heat, and he saw his chance."

"Oh my God!" Jimmy says. "Poor Violet. Everyone else in the café is staring at her. She'll have to leave."

Violet grabbed her school bag and stomped out of the café without looking back at her mother, now in tears.

Chapter Seventeen

"**Poor** Violet!" Jimmy announces, back with Emily. "Jenny thinks all she really wants is for her parents to get back together. She loves being with her mum because she's good fun. They have great times together and she reckons she'd go mad being stuck with her miserable dad, but then she feels sorry for him. She hates to see him sad and lonely and even worries he might top himself if she goes to live with Mum. Also, she's cross about Mum telling lies about domestic violence going on before the sugar puff affair."

"So?" questions Emily. "Do you two guys have an answer?" She sees Sarah give Violet a hug when tears appear in the older girl's eyes.

"The Roo Club!"

"The Roo Club?"

"Yeah! Violet's problem is *their* problem now. Her parents'. She should get *them* to come along to the Roo Club one Friday. We might make them see sense. They have an obligation to their daughter, having brought her into the world. *She's* the victim, whatever else is going on."

"Oh, my wise big brother! What would I do without you?"

"You might've walked into that pond on Hampstead Heath with stones in your pockets!"

"Like Virginia Woolf? Don't rub it in."

"Ask Sarah to suggest my idea to Violet. And tell her

about Kami."

"D'you think *she* should become a member of the Roo Club too? Little Sarah?"

"Most definitely!" agrees Jimmy. "If nothing else, it might put a stop to what's going on between her and Sam."

*****

"I'll do my best," Violet says, later, to little Sarah after the younger girl tells her she absolutely *must* bring both her parents to her school Friday lunch time to get the Roo Club to sort them out.

"I'll be there too," Sarah reassures the older girl. "In case you need me and Claribel."

Clutching Claribel, Sarah gets down off Violet's lap and goes over to where Sam and Kami are seated in conversation.

"Has she told you?" Sarah asks Kami.

"Told me what?"

"That our dad will fix the broken phone for you."

"Not yet," admits Sam. "But I was about to–"

"Oh, big sisters can be so annoying!" interrupts Sarah. "Our dad can fix anything to do with computers and stuff. Mum says he's a wizard. She's got rheumatoid arthritis really bad, you know."

"No, I didn't know. I'm so sorry," Kami says.

"May I sit on you lap?" asks Sarah.

"Of course," replies Kami before helping the child up onto her lap.

"This is Claribel," Sarah says, showing Kami the doll.

"Hello Claribel."

"She wants to know what pervert means. Sam says your brother's a pervert and that's why the phone has to be fixed."

Kami looks at Sam. Sam looks at Emily who turns to her granny who merely offers to go and get more muffins from the kitchen. Four heads, including Sarah's, then turn to face Lingling.

"It means..." begins Lingling looking thoughtful, "...It means doing such bad things to girls like Kami that he'll never be allowed any muffins again in his whole life."

"Things like touching Kami where he shouldn't," adds Emily.

"Why would he want to do that?" asks Sarah.

"Because he's a pervert," explains Sam, coming full circle. "We'll help Kami won't we, Sarah?"

Emily's Granny reappears with an empty plate.

"All gone, I'm afraid. You girls must've been hungry!"

"We've gotta help Kami if we're going to get more muffins," continues Sam. "You and I are gonna ask Dad tonight, aren't we, Sarah!?"

"Bags I do the asking!" insists Sarah.

Sam somehow refrains from saying, 'Because he'll only listen to you!' Instead, she hi-fives with her little sister who promptly gives the older girl a big hug.

*****

Lingling's phone buzzes. She can barely contain her excitement when she sees her father's joyful face appear on the mobile screen.

"Baba! My friends are all here waiting for you. See!"

She holds up the phone, flipping the camera for the man to take in all those grinning faces. Mr Tan waves and the faces' owners wave back. Lingling reverses the camera lens to talk to her dad, first in Mandarin, then in English.

"I'm in the taxi," he replies. "The driver thinks it'll only take an hour. See you soon."

Mr Tan blows his daughter a kiss, the phone is turned off. Almost exactly one hour later, the front door bell rings. Lingling runs to the door and flings it open. Father and daughter collapse, sobbing, into each other's arms. Lingling turns around on feeling someone tap her on the back. It's Sarah, holding Claribel.

"Hello, Mr Sir," the child says. "I'm Sarah and this is Claribel. She knows all about perverts."

"Then she's cleverer than me," Mr Tan responds, stooping to shake Sarah's free hand. "Can she take me to see Emily's granny, please. I have to thank her."

"Thank her for what? More muffins?" the child asks.

"No, not muffins. For persuading the Chinese government to set me free."

"There's a boy in my class who set his pet rabbit free on Hampstead Heath," Sarah tells Lingling's dad as she ushers him towards the sitting room. "It was leaving droppings all over their new carpet and his dad said he'd have the rabbit put down if it didn't stop doing that and it didn't stop so Harry took it to the Heath and set it free instead of getting put down." Sarah looks puzzled. "Will Emily's granny set you free on the Heath then?" the child asks.

"Something like that," is the man's response.

Emily appears in the hallway.

"I'm Emily," she says. "Come and meet my gran, Mr Tan."

As Lingling lugs her father's suitcase indoors, Emily takes Mr Tan into the sitting room to introduce him to the ageing pianist whose past generosity, in all probability, saved the man from a lingering death in a prison cell somewhere on Mainland China. A place where torture was the norm. In the sitting room, Kami, Violet and Sam stand up to acknowledge the man as he approaches Mabel.

"The greatest living Beethoven pianist, Lingling tells me," he says, giving a little bow and offering his hand.

"A pleasure," the old lady declares, shaking the man's hand.

"But for you, I'd still be rotting in jail," Mr Tan assures her.

"When you've done nothing wrong? That's what I told my contact. Promised not to reveal his name. But I told him, if you weren't set free I'd go public. About certain things I know." She tapped her head with her forefinger. "Things concerning their leader best kept secret from others in the Politburo of the Chinese Communist Party. Wheels within wheels, ay?"

"Do wheels really have wheels inside them?" asks

Sarah standing, with Claribel, behind Lingling's dad. "Oh, and by the way, Emily's granny is also the best maker of muffins. Ever! And I really mean it."

"Emily... look in freezer. You might discover more muffins for Mr Tan, hidden away somewhere."

As Emily leaves the room, she overhears Sarah ask Mr Tan why he gave his daughter a funny name like 'Lingling', and outside the door she pauses to hear the man's answer.

"Not funny in Chinese," he replies. "For a girl it means 'Chimes of Jade'. Jade is a very precious stone."

"Oh! Can boys be called Lingling too, then?"

"Of course. But for them it means 'dawn'. Like when you wake up."

"Is that because boys are too lazy to wake up in the morning?"

"I don't think so. But what does *your* name mean, Sarah?"

Emily grins on hearing the child's answer.

"It means a girl who likes muffins."

Chapter Eighteen

"**She's** really cute," Jimmy says as Emily defrosts a bag of muffins that she finds in their granny's freezer.

"I cannot believe she's as mean as Sam says. Perhaps it's the other round like their dad seems to think," Emily suggests.

"Sam being mean to Sarah? Only one way of finding out," declares Jimmy. "Either way, it needs sorting to get their dad's full co-operation."

*****

Whilst Sarah sits on Mr Tan's lap to tell him the life history of Claribel who, she explains, is the 'cleverest doll in the whole world', Emily sits beside Sam, waiting for that opportunity for her brother to...

Za-a-a-p!

Jimmy and Jenny, holding hands, are in there in a flash when Emily's friend looks coldly back at her after being told what a sweet little sister she has...

"It's chilly here," observes Jimmy as the imaginary friends flounder together in the young clarinetist's hippocampus.

A light is turned on...

Sam had Claribel the doll in her hand. Jimmy hears a child's voice calling out,

"Dad, I can't find Claribel. I'm not going to school without her. I'll not learn anything. Can you help me look?"

"Sarah, I'm really busy helping sort out Mum before

going to work. Can't you get Sam to help you?"

"I tried, but she's too busy too. She says she's still doing her homework."

"Before going to school?"

"Yes!"

Jimmy watches, unseen, as Sam quickly stuffed Claribel into her school bag and went to the bathroom to brush her teeth. She swept past Sarah, now in tears, rummaging through the laundry basket on the landing, still looking for her little doll.

"Not found her yet?" Sam asked her little sister. "Oh dear, you might have to go to school on your own today."

"I can't, I can't!" cried Sarah.

"I think we've seen enough," Jenny whispers to Jimmy. He agrees, and they return to his sister's head in the Vale of Health.

"Sarah isn't Sam's problem," he tells Emily. "Sam is."

"How come?"

"The green-eyed monster."

"The who-what?"

"Jealousy."

"I don't understand."

"Jenny and I just saw Sam hiding Claribel in her school bag when her little sister was in tears looking for the doll."

"So... Sarah complaining to her dad that Sam's being mean to her is true after all. But why on earth is she jealous of her baby sister?"

"Oh Emily, can't you see? Being an only child, you get all the attention. Think of Sam's dad there. His wife needs constant help from him, he's working full-time, and, yes, small children like Sarah need a lot of looking after and her mum can't do it. Sam feels left out. On her own, like."

"So... sorting out the broken phone *together* with Sarah and their dad might fix things?"

"Not might. Will!"

*****

Kami, Sam and Emily are hanging out together, midmorning break. Sam looks at Emily. Jimmy seizes his chance and grabs Jenny's hand. In a flash they're inside the other girl's hippocampus...

*****

Sam's holding the broken i-Phone. She and Sarah, with Claribel on her lap, are seated at the breakfast table whilst their dad prepares something for their mum confined to her bedroom as all her joints had seized up. It seems the woman even had to be helped to the bathroom.

"Dad?" asked Sam, looking at her father. "We need your help."

"What with? If it's maths, I'm just too busy right now. Sorry."

"Not maths. It's about perverts," offered Sarah.

The girls' dad stopped what he was doing and looked at his daughters.

"What?" he asked, his face grim with worry.

"There's a pervert on the phone Sam's holding, but

they can't catch him 'cos the phone's broken," the younger girl explained.

The father sat down next to Sam and took the phone from his daughter.

"Whose phone is this?" he asked, touching the fractured screen.

"Kami's. A friend at school," replied Sam.

"*My* friend too!" Sarah insisted. "And her brother's a pervert and it's on the phone but he threw it out of the window. With a kangaroo."

A smile appeared on the man's face.

"A kangaroo, ay?"

"Yes," affirmed Sam. "A soft, toy one."

"Kami's Australian aunt gave it to her," Sarah explained. "Called Joey. The kangaroo. Not the aunt. The phone was in its pouch to record the pervert brother doing bad things, but he threw it out the window and broke it. The phone. Not the kangaroo."

"She's telling the truth," Sam said. "Kami says her brother does things to her when their parents are out."

The father's smile was gone. He looked at Sam.

"What sort of things?"

Sam remained silent.

"Bad things," offered Sarah. "Do *you* know what a pervert is, Dad?"

"This is serious, Sam," the man said, turning the phone over. "Your friend. Kami…" he began.

"Me and Sam are friends, too, now," Sara informed her father. "Honest, we are!"

"Glad to hear it, Sarah. Sam, what did this girl,

Kami, tell you?"

"That he touches her where he shouldn't. In her bedroom. Whenever their parents are out. Which seems to be pretty often."

"And she recorded what happens on this phone?" he asked, holding up the broken phone.

The two girls nodded their heads in unison.

"Poor Kami! I'll see what I can do. Can't promise. Does it turn on?"

"Yes, but that's all," said Sam.

The father turns on the phone but cannot get any further with it. The recording remained hidden on the hard drive.

"Good news... I think. I'll take it to work and text you at school, Sam."

"And me," insisted Sarah. "You can text me as well. I've joined the Roo Club. It's called that because of Joey who got thrown out of the window by Kami's bother."

A smile returned on the man's face.

"I am so glad you two girls are friends again. I know it's been hard on you both, Mum being ill. Hard on all of us."

"*You* could join the Roo Club too," suggested Sarah. "We need a man who you can see. Emily's got a big brother, but nobody can see him."

The father's smile broadened.

"He's a priest," Sarah said.

"Who? Emily's brother that nobody can see?"

"No! Kami's. Not exactly a priest," corrected Sam. "Training to be one."

"The one who—?" began the father.

"The pervert," interrupted Sarah. "*Emily's* brother, he's invisible just like Claribel was before Mummy gave me her old doll. Inside Emily all the time."

*****

"So?" asks Emily. "Your Dad? Can he fix the phone?"

Before Sam can answer, her phone pings. She looks at the screen.

"Talk of the Devil!" she says. "It's Dad. He..." She looks at Kami. "He says to meet him here at lunch time. In Mrs Gray's office."

"Why?" asks Kami.

"He'll have seen the video recording, Sis," Jimmy whispers to Emily. "It'll be bad. I think *you* should go, too. I want to hear what they say."

"My brother wants... I mean *I* want to come too," insists Emily. "Sam's dad'll have seen the video recording. Must be serious."

"I want you with me," agrees Kami. "If it wasn't for you, I'd never have got any evidence."

"And now we know why that brother of yours is a *non-resident* seminarian!"

"Dad thinks he's already a saint. Just goes on and on about how wonderful it'll be to have a priest in the family. 'Your big brother brings us closer to God,' he told me, once."

"He what?" Jimmy says to Emily.

"He what?" Emily asks aloud.

Kami can hold out no longer. She bursts into tears.

"Hug her!" Jimmy tells Emily.

Emily hugs Kami whilst Sam replies to her father before all three set off to Mrs Gray's office to confirm the meeting. The school secretary says a meeting has been set up over lunch break, and that Kami's mother will be present.

Chapter Nineteen

Sam's father is waiting in the school secretary's office. He has the broken phone in one hand and, on his lap, a laptop. He looks up as Emily enters, followed by Sam and Kami. The secretary acknowledges them before going through to inform Mrs Gray they're all there, waiting, bar the girl's mother.

"Which of you two girls is Kami?" Sam's dad asks Emily and Kami. Kami sheepishly raises her hand as if in class. "I'll go in first," he continues. "I need to show Mrs Gray what we've got from the broken phone. All I had to do, Sam, was to connect it to my Mac at work and retrieve data using i-Tunes." He looks at Kami. "Is your mother coming?" he asks.

Kami shrugs her shoulders.

"I spoke with her mother on the phone," the secretary says. "She wanted to know what it's about. I said what Mrs Gray told me to say. That it's a really serious matter that might involve the police."

At which point the door opens, and Mrs Gray's head appears. To Jimmy, watching through his sister's eyes, she looks as though she's just been trampled over by a herd of elephants. Jimmy feels really sorry for her as well as for Kami, and whispers advice to his sister,

'Never take up teaching in a girls' school.'

The woman beckons to Sam's father, and the two disappear into her office. When Kami's mother finally makes an appearance, some fifteen minutes later, her

116

daughter is in tears and being comforted by Sam whilst Jimmy witters on inside Emily's head about the hypocrisy of religion. She wants to argue that, considering the topic, the head teacher's secretary's office of a posh private girls' school is hardly an appropriate place for such a philosophical discussion.

"The perfect place!" insists Jimmy.

"Shut up!" she whispers, thankfully unheard by others as the angry mother of Kami castigates the secretary for taking up her time. She seems too incensed to even notice her daughter being comforted by Sam. The secretary nods her head in Kami's direction. The irate mother turns on the daughter...

"What *have* you been up to now? Your father spends all that money to give you a decent education, and this is how you repay him! Oh, why can't you just be like your brother, huh? Well on his way to becoming a priest and all you can do is to get into serious trouble!"

"Mrs Frobisher, this is hardly the time and place to—"

"Time and place, woman? Who the devil do you think *you* are to tell me about time and place? I could report you to the Board of Governors. In fact, I think I will," she adds with a look of self-satisfaction that adds a grotesque twist to the angered features on her furious face. "I'll get my husband to—"

The door opens, cutting into the woman's sentence like a knife through cheese when Mrs Gray's grim face appears.

"All of you in my office please, except for Kami.

Sally, get a glass of orange juice or something for Kami. We might be a little while."

Frowning, Kami's mother walks briskly through into the head teacher's office, followed by Emily and Sam. She turns and glowers at the two friends.

"Who are these girls? And who's that man?" she asks Mrs Gray, pointing rudely at Sam's father.

Without answering, Mrs Gray pulls up a chair for Kami's mother. The girls remain standing. Mrs Gray then turns around Sam's father's laptop, open on her desktop, so that it faces the accusatory mother. She clicks on 'play', before, over the woman's shoulder, Sam and Emily, with Jimmy inside the latter's head, witness a scene that should give even the most uncaring of mothers nightmares. Mrs Frobisher's jaw drops as, on the screen, she sees her half-naked, beloved son, the apple of his father's eye, force his sister to put on a pair of sexy knickers, whilst calling her 'Knickers', then lie beside him on her bed and demand that she touch him where only a wife should touch a husband.

Silent, she stands up and appears about to leave the room, but Sam and Emily stand in her way. She turns to look at the girls' head teacher, seemingly unable to speak.

"Please, Mrs Frobisher, do sit down. We need to talk. The only crime your daughter has committed is to show quite remarkable bravery. This video footage was rescued from a broken i-Phone loaned to your daughter by the mother of one of these two girls. She's a doctor and wanted to go straight to the police on hearing what your son was putting his young sister through. She loaned the phone to your daughter because the girl was too frightened to tell you and your husband. She thought you'd never believe her if she were to tell the truth. So, they all agreed to provide evidence for the police. Where we take things from here depends very much on Kami. I wanted to know your response before asking your daughter in."

Mrs Frobisher, visibly shaken, sits down.

"I..." she begins but appears unable to come out with anything more than that. Finally, she speaks,

"I... I just don't know what to say. Can you prove that's real? I mean, I've heard you can do anything with AI, these days. That'll be it, won't it? AI?"

"Ask Mr Watling here. He's an IT specialist. His daughter, Sam there, is one of your daughter's friends."

"Yes. I've heard of Sam. And the other girl. Belinda."

"That's Emily, not Belinda. It's *her* mother who's the doctor who had the foresight to lend her phone to Kami."

Mrs Frobisher looks briefly over her shoulder at the girls, then at Sam's father.

"It'll be AI, won't it?" she asks pleadingly.

The man shakes his head.

"No way," he says. "I can tell. I won't bore you with the technical details of how, but the Police Forensics team will agree with me, of this I am certain."

"Police?"

"It's up to your daughter. Shall I ask her in?"

Mrs Frobisher nods. Mrs Gray calls her secretary on the phone to bring Kami through into her office. Mr Watling, Sam's father, gets up to relinquish his chair for the abused girl as she enters the room. Mrs Frobisher turns again to look at her daughter and the other two girls who both step aside for Kami to pass by. When the mother's eyes make contact with Emily's, Jimmy grabs Jenny's hand...

"Now!" he whispers.

*****

"She must've known," Jimmy says as he and Jenny find themselves whirling and twirling in all directions like frenzied ballet dancers. It's not dark. Just colourless, featureless. Difficult to make out anything as they're blown and buffeted about by what could only be described, outside Mrs Frobisher's hippocampus, as 'wind'. The words 'hot air' come to mind for Jimmy as he recalls the woman's reaction to seeing her own daughter being sexually abused by her adored son.

A sudden flash of colours... brightness...

A dining room. Exceedingly posh, but somewhat old-fashioned. Seated on one side of a large, polished oak dining table is the woman inside whose head Jimmy and Jenny are watching Nature's recording of an event that happened, although when, they have no idea. Opposite Mrs Frobisher sits Kami looking as lovely as an orchid flower and wearing a purple and white dress that shows off her womanly young figure to perfection. On the table is a spread of dishes so tempting that Jimmy would have rushed forward, grabbed a plate and started tucking in, had it been in real time.

The door opened. A large-bellied, balding man with a grey moustache, wearing a suit and tie, and a crocodilian smile, entered. He stepped aside for a younger man, possibly early twenties and also immaculately dressed. A man Jimmy last saw with nothing on below the waist. The older man held out his hand as though offering up the vision beheld by Kami's brother as a gift. A vision that included the younger man's fifteen-year-old sister.

"In your honour, son. For being accepted into the seminary. Your first step towards becoming a priest. A man of God. And a first in our family. So..."

The older man led his son to the head of the table and pulled back a chair.

"Nothing less than the place of honour for you, son. Sit down. Please."

The young man sat down, grinning like the Cheshire Cat, whilst his father took his place at the opposite end of the table. There was a small bell there. He picked this up and rang it. A middle-aged woman, dressed as a maid, entered and stood in obedient servitude, hands folded in front of her.

"Your aunt wanted to be here to serve her beloved nephew at the beginning of his journey towards sainthood. Mark, will you do the honours and say grace, please."

"What male chauvinist bastards!" Jenny whispers.

In the same voice that had, in another

hippocampus, ordered the young girl seated at the table to touch a certain part of his anatomy, as later shown to the man's mother in Mrs Gray's office, Mark said grace. In Latin.

"Thank you, Mark. Isabel, would you care to serve your distinguished nephew? This is, indeed, a momentous occasion."

"Oh my God," whispered Jimmy to Jenny. "Did you see that lecherous look on his face when that Mark bloke looked at his sister?"

"I really don't think she knew," Jenny says of the mother who, inside her own hippocampus, appeared as the quietly subservient wife in a male-dominated world.

"What would Mother Earth make of this?" asks Jimmy.

"Turn humans into aphids, perhaps? *Their* females reproduce asexually. It's called parthenogenesis. We've seen enough, I think," replies Jenny. "It's all up to Kami, now."

*****

"Her mother's a victim too," Jimmy tells Emily. "She just doesn't want to believe the recording. It shows that she's been living in a lie. She's got to face up to the truth."

"It's not true, is it, Kami?" the mother asks her daughter, as though aware of Jimmy's silent whisperings. "It can't be. Has to be AI. Who would do such a thing to us?"

"I thought he was going to rape me," is Kami's answer in a voice that is barely audible.

"Mrs Frobisher," begins the head teacher, "I know how difficult this must be for you, but I do have to ask. Were you ever aware that this was going on? What you've just seen?"

Kami's mother shakes her head. Slowly, she gets up, and puts her arms around her daughter. Kami starts to cry. Mrs Frobisher strokes her hair and holds her close.

"And do you think your father knew, Kami?"

"I don't think so."

"Hmm!?" wonders Jimmy, having seen that pompous man, in action, inside his wife's hippocampus.

"Mrs Frobisher, you must realise how serious this is. The implications are enormous. But here and now we must decide what's best for your daughter. You heard what Kami said. She was terrified, the poor girl. It's up to *her* whether or not we refer the matter to the police. Please, both of you, sit down. So we can talk things over."

Kami and her mother sit down.

"First, we must thank Kami's two friends here for bringing this to light, and for helping her," continues Mrs Gray. She focuses her wise and friendly eyes on Kami. Kami turns to look at Emily and Sam, still standing, like sentinels, by the door.

"Thank you," she says. She looks at Sam's father. "And you, sir."

"Mr Watling, please," the man says. "I cannot say it was a pleasure, but what I did what clearly had to be done." He turns to face the head teacher. "Whatever

Kami decides, Sam and I will support her."

"Kami?" Mrs Gray looks at the girl. "We know what happened. Then." She points to the laptop. "Were there other times?"

Kami, now staring at her feet, nods.

"For how long?"

"Since primary school," she replies, still looking at her feet.

Mrs Frobisher claps her hand over her mouth in shock.

"He used to spank my bottom. Lots of times. Pulled my skirt up. Was forever finding excuses to do it. I knew it was wrong, but he used to say I'd be in serious trouble if he told you and dad. And that you'd take my rabbit away. Then, after deciding to become a priest... it was like he had God's blessing. Began touching me where he shouldn't."

All the time, Mrs Frobisher sits, as though glued to her chair, hand over mouth, just staring at her daughter.

Kami shakes her head.

"No police," she says. She looks up at Mr Watling. "Will you come with me and Sam and Emily to the seminary? To tell them. Show them. What Mark's really like."

"Of course I will, Kami. In the name of God, huh?" the man replies. He looks at his watch, then at Mrs Frobisher. "Do we know where the seminary is?"

The woman gives him the details. He goes to his laptop, types these in then turns the laptop around to face the head teacher.

"There's a phone number. Call it, please. Tell them I'll be there to see the Spiritual Director before two o'clock. With Kami and her friends. If not him, someone who has functioning ears to hear what Kami's brother is getting up to. I won't take 'No' for an answer. It's either the seminary or the police."

He looks at Mrs Frobisher.

"You?" he questions.

"Not without my husband," she replies.

"Scared of him?" Jimmy whispers to Emily. His sister says nothing.

Clearly angered, Sam's father beckons Sam, Kami and Emily to follow him.

"And thank you, Mrs Gray. Truly. I didn't expect such understanding," he says.

The woman smiles.

"We head teachers are human. Nowadays. Unlike in your time, I expect. And *I'll* be spending time here with Kami's mother. She's in shock. Understandably. Thank you for coming and being so open with me, Mr Watling. And believe me, your daughter, Sam, is a credit to you. You must be *so* proud of her."

Mr Watling glances sheepishly at his daughter as if suddenly realising what an amazing girl Sam is. Not only musically gifted, but showing a degree compassion unusual in a teenager.

He and the three girls leave together and make haste, on the underground, to the seminary.

Chapter Twenty

"**I** really don't think–" begins the priest, blocking their entrance to the seminary as the girls and Sam's father stand in the street demanding admission.

"That's *your* problem, not mine," interrupted Mr Watling. "If you did try thinking, maybe you might realise what a certain non-resident seminarian of yours has been up to." He holds up his laptop. "It's all here, and I demand to see the Spiritual Director. Now!"

"I think I should call the police."

"I, too, think you should, but the seminarian's sister has gone for the softer option. Your Spiritual Director. Or perhaps the nearest bishop?"

"I–"

Mr Watling takes out his mobile phone and hands it to the priest.

"The police or your Spiritual Director. I've told you *my* preference, but you, too, may wish to respect the young lady's request to see her brother's Spiritual Director instead of the police. How would a jail sentence for one of your seminarians for sexual abuse of his young sister be perceived by the Vatican?"

"Brother?" queries the priest.

"Brother," the other man replies. "Not your kind of 'brother'. Rather, the kind that sees his young sister as an easy target for his abnormal sexual desires. As you see," Mr Watling points to Kami, again on the verge of tears, "she's only a schoolgirl. Her head teacher left a message for the top guy in this outfit."

"Somehow I don't think Sam's family are Catholic," Jimmy whispers to Emily.

"They're not!" she exclaims aloud.

"All heads turn to look at Emily.

"Not what?"

Quick thinking...

"Girls' brothers are not the same as, erm... as religious brothers." Those meaningless words that just pop out of Emily's mouth have the effect of a guillotine cutting off any further exchange between Mr Watling and the priest. The latter stands back, and, head bowed, allows the three girls and Sam's father to pass on through into the building.

"Wow! exclaims Jimmy. Sounds of recorded, chanting, male voices fill an entrance hall dominated by a huge painting of the Crucifixion.

"A reproduction of the famous Grünewald," says the priest, proudly. "Rather nice, isn't it."

"It's so peaceful here," whispers Jimmy. A group of young seminarians appear at the top of the stairs. Their conversation ceases abruptly as their eyes fix on the outsider accompanied by three schoolgirls."

"They look pretty normal to me," whispers Jimmy. "Not like perverts."

Emily whispers back, inside her head.

"They probably are," she says. "Normal, that is. They can't all be like Kami's brother."

"Hope not! But I do like it here. So peaceful."

"Thinking of becoming a priest then, big brother."

"Probably not. If they can't marry."

"Marry?" It has never once occurred to Emily that Jimmy would one day wish for a life of his own, and a lifelong companion other than herself. She has only ever thought of him as being there, inside her head, to help *her*. Support *her*. She feels scared. Sure, things are so much better now since having three of her friends back, but Belinda was still out there, like a large, black spider lurking in a hidden web.

They're taken along a corridor to a door. The priest knocks on the door, opens it, slightly, and peers inside to ask whether whoever it is beyond the door is,

"...Expecting a gentleman and three... erm...?"

He turns around to take in the three pretty girls. His face turns beetroot.

"And three schoolgirls? In their uniform."

"Mr Watling? Plus the girl in question and two others. Yes, I am. Expecting them, that is. Please, show them in, Father O'Brian."

Moments later, inside an office adorned with a crucifix and more religious painting on its walls, four chairs are provided for the girls and for Sam's father. A priest, sitting behind a tidy desk, looks up at them. A look that radiates compassion... concern.

"This guy's not only normal, but *nice* normal," whispers Jimmy.

"Which of you girls is Kami?" the Director asks.

Kami raises her hand, again as if in class.

"Your head teacher has put me in the picture, and I have already spoken with your mother. I am, of course, deeply concerned that one of our very own seminarians, who showed so much spiritual gift, behaved as he did."

Mr Watling places the laptop on the desk in front of the priest who merely waves his hand to indicate that he has no interest in seeing the video footage. Sam's father takes back the laptop and rests it on his knees.

"Kami, I'm glad you came to me, first, but would quite understand should you wish to involve the police."

The girl shakes her head. The Director addresses Sam's father again,

"With immediate effect, Mark Frobisher's position with us, as a trainee priest, is terminated. I have already arranged his transfer to a retreat in the country. For spiritual guidance. We must all hope he will truly and sincerely seek God's forgiveness. And, in time, yours too, Kami. Your father has been advised of the graveness of the matter. Should your brother make any attempt to contact you, by any means, please let me know, and the police will most certainly be alerted."

The Director asks whether Kami has any questions. She shakes her head.

"I have one for you, young lady. Your name. I was wondering how a Catholic girl like you has a Japanese name."

Kami smiles.

"My dad was on business in Japan when Mum was pregnant with me. He met a Japanese guy at church. They got talking after mass. Got round to discussing names for me as my parents couldn't decide, and..." The girl paused.

"And you got named 'Kami'. Do you know what the name means in Japanese?"

"No idea."

"In Shinto, which isn't exactly a religion so you can be Catholic and believe in Shinto, 'kami' is like a spirit that pervades everything in the Universe."

Emily speaks up.

"It means you'll go far, Kami," she says. She looks at the Director. "She's a brilliant violinist, you know. Spot on with the Schubert sonatinas. I used to accompany her."

"*Used* to?" questions the Director.

In reply, Emily holds up her injured hand.

"Oh... I am sorry. How...?"

"Belinda," explains Kami. "And me and Sam got taken in by her too. She's evil. Like my brother."

"Evil? I don't believe that. Strayed from the path of righteousness, maybe. Have you not wondered why? Perhaps someone can one day make this girl, Belinda, see the 'Light'. As you have hopefully done with your brother through your brave action. Your parents named you well, young lady."

The Director rises from his chair. A small man with a huge heart.

"I have work to do, now. Attempt to make a bunch of wayward seminarians as wise and Godly as you three girls. And thank you, Kami, for helping to rescue one of our flock from the Devil's embrace."

The man smiles, and Kami smiles back at him, together with her two friends. Jimmy even smiles inside his sister's head, and on their way out of the building he asks her whether she'd ever thought about becoming Catholic, like Kami.

"And she does have lovely blue eyes," he adds.

"Shut up!" Emily whispers.

"Why did you just say, 'Shut up!', Em?" asks Sam, grinning. "No one said anything."

Emily shrugs her shoulders but realises, in a flash, why Belinda regarded her as weird and turned her friends against her.

"Felt like it," she says, untruthfully.

"Let's say it together," suggests Kami, grinning. "All of us. You as well, Mr Watling. As loud as we can. Like we're shouting at the Devil who's twisted my big brother and turned him into a monster."

Together, Sam's father included, they all stop, stand still in the street outside the seminary and, together, shout out, "Shut up!"

An old lady, bent like a question mark, and taking her little chihuahua for a walk on the opposite side of the street, also stops, looks at them, says something to her dog, then walks on.

"Just reassuring the little animal that we weren't shouting at him?" Jimmy suggests.

"Or her?" questions Emily in silence. "Couldn't really tell from this side of the street, but she did look a little worried."

Chapter Twenty-one

"**Good** of Mrs Gray to ask Vi's mum and dad to show up at the Roo Club today," Jimmy says to Emily as she prepares her school bag on Friday morning. "Can you imagine what it's like for your friend to have parents always at each other hammer and tongs?"

"No, I can't," says Emily, aloud, in the safety of her bedroom.

Safety?

A privilege denied Kami for so long because of her brother. Emily recalls thinking, after the meeting at school with Sam's dad, Kami, Mrs Frobisher and Mrs Gray, how lucky *she* is to have a caring brother inside her head rather than an uncaring one, outside, in the real world. "Let's hope something will come of it now he's been sent packing by that priest," she adds. "And let's hope the same's true for poor Vi and her bickering parents."

"It will be. If little Sarah appears on Friday, *she'll* sort them out, for sure!"

"With Claribel?"

Jimmy laughs that comforting laugh of his.

"Of course! Claribel will most certainly make those two parents see sense!"

*****

When Emily arrives with Lingling, during lunch break, at the school secretary's office, for the weekly Friday Roo Club meeting, with Jimmy and Jenny tagging along inside her head, she's surprised to see it empty.

"Where is everyone?" Lingling asks.

The chatter of voices audible through wall between Mrs Gray's office and her secretary's gives Jimmy the answer.

"In the boss's office," he whispers.

"In the boss's office?" questions the sister.

The door opens and Mrs Gray's friendly face peers at them from the other side.

"We're all in my office," she says. "My secretary's one isn't big enough. The way things are going, you'll soon need to use the assembly hall. You won't mind if I attend your Roo Club meeting today, will you, Emily? I think I might learn a thing or two from you girls!"

"Are Vi's parents here?"

"Indeed, they are. Plus, that amazing little sister of Sam's with, erm..." She turns her head to seek out Sarah happily chatting away.

"Claribel!" a high-pitched voice calls out. "She's called Claribel."

"Claribel," Mrs Gray affirms. "Mr Watling wanted to come too but couldn't take time off from his work. I'm trying to persuade him to get help at home with his invalid wife, but he's a proud man. Likes to do everything himself, it seems."

"You can say that again!" agrees Sam. Mrs Gray steps back to allow the two girls into her office.

"Emily and Lingling, can I introduce you to Violet's parents, Mr and Mrs Savage?"

The man gets up. The woman, tight-lipped, remains

seated.

"Hello!" the girls greet, in unison.

"Hello there," responds Mr Savage. His wife merely nods.

Mrs Gray addresses Emily,

"First, Emily, I believe there is overwhelming support for your granny to become an honorary member of your club. But I'll leave the rest of the meeting in your capable hands. Think of me as an invisible observer."

Invisible? Like Jimmy and Jenny, Emily would like to say, but doesn't.

Emily and Lingling take the only two empty seats left in their head teacher's office. All eyes are on Emily. Inside the girl, Jimmy's and Jenny's ears are pricked.

Emily addresses Violet's parents,

"Thank you so much for coming. Must have been difficult for both of you to take time off from work, and we really appreciate it. But we're all so worried about Violet. She..."

Emily's mind goes blank. What on earth can she say without being intrusive into their private, family affairs? Jimmy, though, being invisible to them has no problem with being blunt and to the point.

"She loves them both..." he whispers to his sister.

"She loves you both very much," Emily says out loud, "But..."

"But feels she's being torn apart having to choose between you," continues Jimmy. "Jenny's suggestion."

"But she feels she's being torn apart having to

choose between her mum and her dad," says Emily. "Jenny's... erm..." Her mind goes blank again.

Jimmy? Help me, Jimmy!

"Try, 'Jenny's a friend of my mum in the same boat as Mrs Savage. Her daughter was also being torn apart but was saved when the mum and dad got together again. Made a pact to always both be there for their daughter."

Emily repeats her brother's suggestion. A way out of the embarrassment of having come out with Jenny's name.

"Say this daughter is now doing brilliantly at uni and they all have great times together as a family."

Again, Emily lies as told to by her big brother, then takes in the circle of faces, fixed on her, for some sort of a response. Sarah's hand shoots up.

"Claribel agrees. She doesn't want Violet to be sad any longer."

"Vi?" questions Emily of her friend, sitting quietly between her parents. Jimmy is reminded of a sandwich, the pretty girl with lovely sleek black hair being the delicious filling in between two slices of stale bread.

"I only want *that* thing, Emily. What happened to the daughter of your mum's friend? All getting back together again. As a family. No more fighting."

"What about the sugar puffs?" asks Sarah. "Claribel wants to know about them."

Mr Savage, half-laughing, half in tears, tells Sarah that the sugar puffs were a wake-up call that he and Mrs Savage badly needed.

"Claribel thinks it's a waste of sugar puffs to put them on your head."

"Claribel's right," affirms Mr Savage. "Actually, young lady, Mrs Savage and I did meet up together this morning before coming here." He puts his arm around Violet. "We're determined to start over. Make it work. Right, Mrs Savage?"

Mrs Savage nods. She looks at Emily.

Z-z-z-zap!

Jimmy and Jenny are inside her hippocampus. Cold, dark and dingy till...

*****

Another office. Much like the school secretary's office. In front of a desktop computer sits Mrs Savage. Somehow, she looks younger.

"Maybe it's her makeup?" queries Jimmy.

"No! It'll be because of what's on the other side of that door there," suggests Emily.

Jimmy can't fail to notice how the woman, not bad looking for one in her middle years, keeps glancing at the door to the adjoining room as though expecting something life-changing to suddenly appear from the other side of it.

The door opened. A man appeared.

"Wow!" exclaims Jenny. "I may be seventy-seven, but I still know a *real* man when I see one."

Jimmy, however, is unimpressed.

"Looks more like an out-of-work actor to me. Let's see what he comes up with."

The man walked over to the secretary's desk with

the confidence of a panther. He put an arm across Mrs Savage's shoulders as he peered at the computer screen. Still apparently focusing on the screen, he put his face down close to his secretary's neck and drew in a long and audible breath through a perfectly proportioned, aquiline nose. His free hand slipped into his pocket to take out a small bottle of perfume which he placed on the desk in front of Mrs Savage.

"Ralph Lauren," he said. "It's called 'Romance'. Like that night we had together before you told me you were leaving him. And when you said it was just like your first time."

"It was, but—"

"But what, Jayne? Free from him, you can have 'it' as often as you want."

"Not that easy. There's our daughter, Violet."

"If she's as beautiful as you, she's all set for the future."

"And Frank. He—"

"He hit you! Remember? I offered to hit him back, but you said you wouldn't have it. Said it was between you and him. So, I told you to go to the police. Fat lot they did, just giving him a caution." The man clenched the fist that had produced the bottle of perfume. "You should've let me smash his face in, Jayne."

"You're married," the woman announced.

"What of it? So are you. Doesn't stop us having a good time, does it?"

"Good time? Are there others like me? For you?"

The man stepped back.

"What are you talking about?"

"Am I the only woman you've had an affair with?"

"Such an unpleasant word, 'affair'. Let Nature take her course, I always say to my students. 'Event' is a far better word. A *natural* event. I *want* it. You *need* it. *It* happens."

"Your female students?"

The man stepped stiffly away from his secretary's desk.

"Jayne, I want all those letters done by lunchtime. Okay?"

"Yes, Professor."

Without any further exchange of words, the man returned to his office, closing the door behind him.

"Like her daughter, she's being pulled in two directions as well," says Jenny. "I mean, he is gorgeous."

"As gorgeous as a heap of elephant shit?" suggests Jimmy.

"You're a man," says Jenny, "so you wouldn't understand her dilemma."

"And your seventy-seven and should know better. He's an absolute bastard. Out to get any unsuspecting woman with a weak spot. Calls himself a professor, huh? A 'possessor', more like."

"You're right. But only *this* time! Mostly, it's me that's right."

"Let's get outta here," urges Jimmy. "Before I escape from this hippocampus and strangle the geyser. He doesn't give a damn about poor Vi. Anyway, we'd better get back to the Roo Club. See what's happening."

Back inside Emily, Jimmy informs his sister that Violet's mother's boss is a heap of elephant shit who calls himself a professor and preys on vulnerable females.

"Hate to think how many female students he's bedded," he says. "Jenny thought he has a sexy nose, but to me it looked more like a monkey's dick."

"A monkey's dick!?" exclaims Emily aloud, grinning.

Silence. Everyone looks at her.

"Dictation, I mean," she says. "A monkey's dictation makes no sense. Like... erm... like forcing Violet to choose between her mum and dad."

Mrs Gray rescues the girl.

"That is an unusual way of putting it, Emily. Mr and Mrs Savage will, it seems, think things over. And as Kami says, Violet will forgive *them* if *they* forgive each other."

"Missed that bit," Jimmy whispers to Jenny. "It's not just the eyes, then."

"What?" asks Jenny.

"Kami. Her eyes. Haven't you noticed them?"

"They're there. Where they should be. Why?"

"They're simply gorgeous. *And* she's a lovely nature, too, from what Mrs Gray says. Not like that creep with the monkey dick nose."

Jenny laughs.

"Aquiline," she insists. "But yes, he is a creep of the worst kind. Tell your sister to suggest Vi's mum hands in her notice. There must be vacancies for secretaries all over the place. Mrs Gray might be able to help her."

Emily passes on Jimmy's suggestion to the Roo Club committee after Violet and her parents have left, and Mrs Gray immediately gets on the phone to her husband, a teacher in a nearby boys' school that, she has been informed, is short of a secretary. And after Mrs Gray asks Emily to stay behind in her office, Jimmy seizes the opportunity. He and Jenny agree that there is something quite remarkable about Emily's head teacher and wish to learn more about her.

Chapter Twenty-two

Just Mrs Gray and Emily alone in the head teacher's office. Plus, of course, Jimmy. Jenny left earlier as, according to her, she has urgent business with her long-time imaginary (in *their* dimension) friend, Mabel, who also happens to be Jimmy's grandmother. He's a little anxious about carrying out what's been on his mind since Emily entered that room, for he's never done it without Jenny, but, as the lovely, seventy-seven-year-old teen so often tells him, there has to be a first time for everything.

"Please sit down," Mrs Gray says.

Emily sits. Jimmy reckons he knows what this is about.

"You and Belinda?" the woman asks. She looks pointedly at Emily's bandaged hand.

Emily remains silent.

"Have there been problems?"

Emily shrugs her shoulders but says nothing.

"Before Violet and her parents arrived, Sam and Kami told me there has been bullying going on. Belinda and Ava ganging up against you. Is it true?"

Emily can no longer hold back the tears. Seemingly unable to answer the question, she starts to sob. Mrs Gray pushes a box of tissues in her direction. Emily takes one and wipes her tears.

"I can understand you don't want to be labelled a snitch, but I am trying to promote zero tolerance in my school when it comes to bullying."

"It's my fault."

"What's your fault?"

"I talk funny at times. And I have this..." Emily pauses, as though hesitant to tell her head teacher the truth about Jimmy.

"Yes?"

"This brother, like. Older brother. Only no one else can see him. But I know he's real. Inside me, like."

"And when you talk to him aloud people think you're talking to yourself, right?"

Emily nods.

"Like an imaginary friend, then. Perfectly normal in children. And sometimes continues into the teens. Even adulthood."

"My granny has one too. Called Jenny."

"And your brother's name?"

"Jimmy."

"Does Jimmy help you, sometimes?"

The tears reappear.

"Always."

Jimmy takes his chance when the woman looks into his sister's eyes. Alone in her brain, he soon finds his way to her hippocampus where memories, both long past and recent, beckon to him like street market sellers. One in particular grabs his attention and immediately fills the space in which he finds himself.

*****

Jimmy is in a hospital corridor following signs to the paediatric ward as he watches a replay inside his sister's

142

head teacher's brain.

Mrs Gray, much younger, but easily recognizable, was hurrying along with a man. Her husband? He spoke,

"You really must *not* blame yourself, Christine. She said she was feeling better when you put her to bed. Remember?"

"I should've looked for that rash. Should've known. I'm a teacher, for heaven's sake."

"So am I! Look, it'll not do Amy any good castigating yourself like this. And maybe it's not as bad as we feared when we got the call from the hospital."

Mr and Mrs Gray arrived at the paediatric ward where, straightaway, they were met by the nurse in charge.

"I'm afraid they've taken Amy to Intensive Care. She needs support with her breathing. I think you should go there. The next floor up."

"Is she—?" began Mrs Gray.

"You should go!"

Jimmy senses the fear, the desperation and the vanishing hope in the woman who ran from the ward, followed by her husband, and made for the lift. Arriving at the floor above, the lift door slid open and Mr and Mrs Gray rushed on towards the Intensive Care Unit. Here, they were met by a mask-wearing nurse in theatre scrubs and taken into a small office. Mrs Gray's repeated question, "How is Amy?" remained unanswered.

"Please sit down. I'll fetch the doctor," the nurse

said.

Jimmy wants to shout out what the husband had already said to Emily's head teacher...

"Do not blame yourself!"

But he can't. What he witnesses happened way back in the past judging by the age difference between the two Mrs Grays.

The   doctor appeared at the doorway. A young woman with a mask on and wearing blue scrubs. Looked just like another nurse. She closed the door behind her and sat down on a chair opposite the anxious parents.

"I'm so sorry," she said. "We did everything we could to save Amy, but it had got into her blood stream. Meningococcus."

Mrs Gray collapses up against her husband, sobbing uncontrollably.

"Can we see her?" the man asks.

"I'll ask my consultant."

The doctor left the room and returned moments later with an older woman, also in scrubs. More apologies that the child's life wasn't saved before the parents were taken to see the child's body behind closed curtains. The girl's eyes were also closed, and it almost seemed as though she was just asleep; *fast* asleep, never to wake up again. The parents' grief was harrowing to watch, but Jimmy had learned something. That behind the calm and friendly face of his sister's head teacher was hidden a past of unimaginable tragedy. All the woes of Emily and her friends put together would not come anywhere near the awfulness of losing a young child.

Back with Emily, Jimmy told his sister to keep nothing from Mrs Gray for her past gave her a depth of understanding even greater than that of their doctor parents.

*****

"Jimmy just told me about Amy."

Mrs Gray looks puzzled.

"Amy Fairweather? She's not even in your class. And so mild-tempered I can't even imagine her even bullying a flea."

"Not *her*. *Your* Amy. Who died. From something called..." Emily paused whilst trying to recall what it was that had so cruelly stripped that mysterious thing called life away from her head teacher's little daughter. Jimmy whispered the word inside her...

"Meningococcus," adds Emily. "It got into her bloodstream, Jimmy says."

Mrs Gray just stares at her pupil before coming out with,

"Oh my God. How could he know? That was so long ago."

"Memories. Stored in your hippocampus."

"My what?"

"Hippocampus. My granny's imaginary friend, Jenny, taught Jimmy how to get there through the eyes. It's somewhere in the brain, I think. And as Jimmy and Jenny are from a different dimension—"

"And you and Jimmy share the same parents and grandparents?" interrupts Mrs Gray.

Emily nods.

"Same but different realities. Jimmy keeps getting me to search the internet to find out what reality's all about, but it's kind of way beyond me."

"Me too"

"And being in a different dimension they can go places in this world, unseen, that we'd never think possible."

"You're telling me your imaginary brother found out about my daughter dying just now through travelling around my brain via my eyes?"

"Yes."

"Emily, this is awfully scary. I need a moment to—"

"No, Mrs Gray, it *isn't*. Scary, that is. He, Jenny and other imaginary people can't do you any harm at all. Because they don't really exist in this world. It's only that I can communicate with Jimmy. But not Jenny. She's not real for me, although she can get inside my head, but she is real for Granny, of course. And for Jimmy. Those two share the same reality and can see each other."

"How did this start, Emily?"

"The hippocampus travel thing? After Jimmy met Jenny when I showed up at Granny's in the Vale of Health with him because he dissuaded me from walking into a pond on Parliament Hill Fields with pockets full of stones. Like that writer, Virginia Woolf."

"And who, like Kami, was sexually abused by her brothers. Or half-brothers. From the age of six. But tell me, honestly, has Belinda been bullying you as Kami and Sam both claimed before that Roo Club meeting?"

Emily thinks hard before shaking her head. The delay in her response to her head teacher's question speaks volumes, but her denial of the truth means that the woman is unable to tackle the problem head on. Instead, she comes out with,

"Whatever is or isn't happening between you two girls, I will address bullying at the next school assembly."

Emily looks up at her in alarm having, up until then, kept her eyes firmly focused on her folded hands resting on her lap.

"Using as an excuse the laudable work you girls are doing with your Roo Club to address other girls problems whatever they may be. Thank you, Emily."

As Emily gets up to leave, Mrs Gray makes a comment,

"Some say that inside every bully hides a frightened child. You may not be doing Belinda a service by saying that Kami and Sam are lying."

"Thank you, Mrs Gray," says Emily before leaving the room.

"Why didn't you tell her the truth?" asks Jimmy as his sister heads for her classroom. "She's so kind and understanding."

"Best avoid the subject. Belinda and Ava can go jump in the lake, for all I care."

"Or pond?" queries Jimmy. "Remember Virginia Woolf. Abused, like Kami, by her half-brothers. Maybe you'd be helping Belinda. Not snitching on her."

"I'd rather forget her. Imagine she doesn't exist. Wouldn't that be great? A Belinda-free world?"

"How many more amazing novels might Virginia Woolf have written if she hadn't drowned herself? Could be Belinda's a writer, too?" suggests Jimmy.

"She's certainly not into music. Oh, let's both just shut up about Belinda the bloody Italian pin-up girl!"

Thankfully, Jimmy, who is beginning to annoy Emily, goes silent as she enters the classroom.

Chapter Twenty-three

Friday morning... school assembly.

"It has been brought to my attention that there has been bullying in our school. This is something I deplore. I am aware that girls at the receiving end may not wish to be labelled 'snitches'—a cruel word indeed—but I will remind you that those responsible will face suspension if found out. Also, your very own Roo Club has ears that will listen, away from us teachers, to those girls who are being bullied. From now on, my own ears will be absent from the Roo Club, so do not feel intimidated to share your problems with the girls running the club. They *will* listen to you. They *can* help you..."

"What a woman!" whispers Jimmy as Emily leaves assembly on her way to a maths class.

Friday lunch time, back in Mrs Gray's office, this time without the head teacher. Clearly, the woman felt the Roo Club would have a better chance to root out the bullies in her absence. Sarah and Claribel are there, of course, since Sarah's school is just two streets away. Their presence alone cheers up girls who appear, after waiting in the secretary's office, to pour out their woes to Emily and her friends. Problems ranging from, "I hate my maths teacher!" to "My boyfriend is complaining about my spots". The latter complainant laughs on hearing Sarah say that, according to Claribel, spots only appear on the faces of clever people and that the boyfriend must be stupid if he doesn't have any.

Jimmy, however, complains that he's getting bored, and Emily begins to think the Roo Club is a waste of time until, five minutes before the bell is due to ring, there's a knock on the office door, and the very last student, that lunch time, makes her appearance before the Roo Club committee...

Ava.

"Isn't she one of the bullies?" Jimmy asks Emily in silence. "Comes to confess, ay?"

As though she, too, hears Jimmy, she looks Emily in the eye and says,

"I'm sorry."

"Sit down," says Sam. The girls have decided to take it in turns to 'lead an enquiry' as they term each counselling session, and for Ava it happens to be Sam's turn. Even Sarah and Claribel are on the rota to 'lead'. And separately, for Sam's little sister insists that Claribel sometimes take the lead. "She's very understanding," Sarah informs the committee.

Ava sits, head bent, looking at her lap.

"So were some of us when we came forwards," Sam continues. "Sorry, that is. But that's not what we do here. Criticise. We're here to help you, Ava."

Ava remains silent, still staring down at her empty lap.

"Ask her something," Jimmy says to his sister. Emily's mind goes blank. "Ask her why she never performs at school concerts. You told me you once heard her play a Rachmaninov prelude in the music room and is every bit as good as you are on the piano."

"Your Rachmaninov's brilliant," Emily says aloud. "Why didn't you perform at the concert last term?"

Ava looks at Emily.

"Now," whispers Jenny to Jimmy. In a flash, the imaginary friends are on their way to the half-Russian girl's hippocampus, a dark and soulful place. Then, moments later, they're in a nearby park. Ava is seated on a bench beside Belinda, both in school uniform.

"My dad can help you and your mum," Belinda offers. "I spoke to him last night."

"I'm scared," the other girl said.

"She looks it," whispers Jimmy. "Lovely legs, though."

"Shut up!" whispers Jenny. "Listen. Watch. We're here to help Emily. Not to get a girlfriend for you."

"It'd be so much easier for me if you didn't go on about being seventy-seven."

"Well, I am. And old enough to be your grandmother. Look, we've got to help Ava. She was a good friend of Emily's. Once. We're here to find out what's happening."

"Why?" asks Belinda. "Maybe your dad just got called away. Had to go back to Russia on business, perhaps?"

"Without telling us? Putin has his informants everywhere. Mum told Dad to say nothing about Navalny, but he just went on and on about the man being such a hero, and that Russia would be a great place to live in if he'd become president. Now he's dead. Murdered by Putin's thugs, Dad said."

"Your dad's in business, right?"

"Mmm!"

"What sort?"

"No idea. Just 'business'. But he always told us where he was going, what he was doing. He's a great dad. Honest, he is!"

"And he's vanished without saying anything?"

"It's been two weeks now. Not a word. Then—"

"The money?" questions Belinda.

"Mum says their bank account got emptied. Closed. We're penniless. Mum's English rellies don't have a bean. They're all up North, anyway. My uncle in Oldham hasn't been in touch for years, anyway. He doesn't like Russians. Says they're untrustworthy."

"Dad'll help you, I know he will. Our family's very supportive. My own uncle is rolling in money, even if he is weird."

"Weird?"

"Creepy, more like. I try to avoid him, but he *is* a billionaire, Dad says. And he likes music. Ballet and stuff, anyway."

"Hmm! Girls in leotards, I expect!"

"You could play that Russian song for him, perhaps?"

"The Rachmaninov prelude? That's the problem. I get panic attacks. Ever since I was little. They got worse when Dad started going on about Navalny, and Mum said he could be putting us in peril. No way could I perform for your uncle."

Belinda put her arm around Ava.

"Perhaps she's not that bad," whispers Jimmy.

"Ava?"

"No, Belinda. And she's really good looking. Great boobs."

"Oh, do shut up! We're here to help Ava."

"She's nice, too. And her legs are—"

"Shh! There's something going on. Look!"

Belinda had taken out her mobile and was calling someone.

Her father? Jimmy wonders.

"We must get back to Emily," he says.

Another flash, and Jimmy and Jenny are back in Mrs Gray's office with Emily and the other members of the Roo Club. Sam is asking Ava about her panic attacks, and whether or not she has seen a doctor for help with them.

"Of course I have," answers Ava. "Dad insisted. He really does worry about me. I've tried special pills, but they only made me sleepy. Also relaxation exercises, but they made me worse. Got even more anxious."

"The way you played the opening chords of the C sharp minor Rachmaninov prelude was out of this world," Emily says. "I felt quite jealous when I heard you play."

"You? When you're the very best? And with that famous grandmother of yours?"

"I know about your father disappearing."

"How? I've only told Belinda."

"That's what I'm worried about."

There's a long pause.

"Something's wrong," whispers Jimmy.

"I know," Emily says aloud.

"Know what?" asks Ava, clearly alarmed. "About Dad?"

"I was talking to Jimmy. My brother. He says to beware. Of Belinda. *And* her uncle. Especially her uncle."

"Emily, this has nothing to do with that brother of yours," scolds Sam. "And it's *my* turn to the enquire for Ava, anyway."

"Just saying," responds Emily in her defence.

"No, *I* was saying," insists Jimmy inside his sister's head. "There's something about Belinda and her Italian uncle. Dunno what. Just a feeling I have."

Emily shrugs her shoulders but keeps quiet whilst Sam questions Ava further about her panic attacks.

"Ask her if she was bullied at primary school for being half-Russian," suggests Jimmy.

Spot on! Ava tearfully admits she *was* bullied. Mercilessly. She was labelled the 'Ruski', and her love of classical music didn't help. No other children had heard of Mozart or Bach, and even their teacher probably thought Rachmaninov was a name for cheap vodka. The girl's mother had begged the father to send their daughter to a private school which, back then, they could easily afford, but he insisted Ava should be 'just another member of the Great British public', and 'not stand out'. Even then, he was scared of something for his family. However, the child psychologist finally agreed with the mother. To send her gifted musical daughter to a school where music really counted seemed the best option, and the father backed down. Despite this, the panic attacks continued and, recently, the sudden disappearance of her father, who openly castigated Putin for attacking Ukraine, as well as standing up for Navalny, has affected the girl badly. Hence her appearance at the Roo Club that Friday lunch time.

"Does your mum work?" asks Emily after being prompted to do so by Jimmy.

Ava shook her head.

"My dad might help find her a job," Sam says. "Does she type? Your mum?"

"Before she met my dad, that's what she was. A typist."

"We'll all be on the lookout for typing jobs for your mum, then."

Sarah put her hand up. Sam pointed to her.

"Yes, Sarah?"

"Claribel thinks we should do a charity run," the little sister informed the club. "My school *and* yours. You can get people to spongy thingy you."

"Spongy thingy?" questions Sam.

"Sponsor?" suggests Kami, silent up until that moment.

"That's what Claribel said only I didn't understand the word. Sponsor."

"Asking people to donate money for you to give to Ava's mum if they finish the run," explains Lingling. "What a lovely idea, Sarah."

"Claribel's, not mine."

No one dared to laugh or contradict the child.

"Next Wednesday afternoon on Hampstead Heath?" proposed Sam. All agreed to Sarah's suggestion of a charity run, finishing off at Emily's granny's place in the Vale of Health for 'refreshments'... which was interpreted by all as meaning muffins.

"Good one, Sarah," says Sam, high fiving with her sister. "I am so very proud of you."

Surely, Sarah's smile in response to her sister's remark would have melted even Belinda's icy heart.

Chapter Twenty-four

The following afternoon, preparations are well under way for the Charity Run next Wednesday. After a text message from Sam, towards the end of the Roo Club meeting, the young clarinetist's dad sets up Crowd Funding on a Just Giving webpage. At Emily's school, a special assembly is announced, by Mrs Gray, on Friday afternoon, to tell everyone about the run to be marked out by the school sports teacher. The police have been informed, and Mrs Gray has already consulted her opposite number in Sarah's primary school.

The only person who shows a total lack of interest is Belinda Contini. She seems irritated by the whole idea.

"I told you my dad will fix it with my uncle to get you and you mum some money," she reminds Ava.

"You said he's a creep."

"Ah, but a loaded creep. Is Emily behind this? Or that mysterious brother of hers?"

"No. Sam's little sister, actually."

Ava shows up at Emily's granny's place on the Saturday. Violet insists her mum and dad come too. Together. Emily's parents, as well, appear as the girl's father has the weekend off call.

Granny informs the ''erd', as she calls the assembled crowd in her Cockney accent, that she's been baking all week and has a freezer full of muffins in preparation for the charity event. On hearing that Ava is a gifted pianist who can sight read, she suggests the half-Russian girl take her place for Schubert practice with Lingling whilst others compare notes for the Charity Run.

It was to be called the 'Roo Run' because no one could think of a better name. Flyers and posters are printed by Sarah's and Sam's dad and distributed by all. Even the local press and news media have been informed.

Then, whilst Lingling are playing the Schubert for the third time that afternoon—a sound so heavenly that no one complains—Kami lets the cat out of the bag. Or rather, the *brother* out of the *brain*.

"Emily's imaginary brother has been so helpful to all of us," she tells Emily's parents."

"Her what?"

Kami looks at Emily. Emily just looks embarrassed. Granny breaks the ice.

"Just something we've shared over the years," she says. "Asked Emily to keep it secret, and never told you 'cos of the brother's name. Where she got this from I don't know, but just recently he and my childhood imaginary friend, Jenny, seem to have got together."

"Jimmy," says Emily, looking at her mother. "I've always called him Jimmy."

Tears appear in the mother's eyes as she sits looking at her daughter. Emily's dad, sitting beside her mum, takes hold of her hand.

"I'm so sorry we never told you, Emily."

"Told me what."

"About your brother. James. He'd be seventeen, turning eighteen, had he survived."

"What are you taking about?"

Alone, Jimmy slips from Emily into his mother, where, in the woman's hippocampus he immediately finds himself, as with his sister's head teacher, inside a hospital, only this time in a neonatal unit.

His mother and father, again much younger and also in tears, stood side by side in front of an incubator. One of several, but the small infant lying inside this one, wearing only a tiny nappy, was motionless, unlike the babies in other incubators whose little limbs jerked and kicked as their searching eyes took in the wonder of modern medicine happening all around them. But science had been unable to save one special life. The life of a newly born called, according to what was written on the tag encircling its little ankle, 'James'.

"I'm so sorry we couldn't save him," a nurse told Jimmy's parents as, speechless, they held on to each other.

So that's me. I am, or rather was, real. Emily is my sister. Not just imaginary.

Thoughts fluttered about like crazed butterflies inside Jimmy's invisible head.

If only I could get out of this hippocampus into that hospital to tell my parents, back then, that it's going to be all right. That they will still have a son. And that because of their daughter, not yet born, I will see them again. Through her eyes.

Also now in tears, Jimmy returns to his granny's

159

place. To tell his sister not to blame their parents for keeping quiet about the fact that all along she's had an elder brother who only spent a few fraught hours in this world before, a little over two years later, returning from another reality to help look after his newborn baby sister, for he felt this was the very least he could do for his grieving mother and father.

"Please don't blame them for not telling you," Jimmy implores Emily. "They must have been so over the moon to have a healthy happy baby when you arrived. Why would you have to know? Granny must have sworn secrecy about me, too. Just like she swore secrecy with you not to tell them that you have an imaginary brother called 'Jimmy'. It would only have hurt them even more if they couldn't see me. Couldn't hold me. Just let them think it's pure coincidence that you've always called me 'Jimmy'."

"It's all right, Mum. Just coincidence I've always called my imaginary brother 'Jimmy'. Anyway, why *should* you have told me I have a real brother? What difference would it have made?"

"He only lived a few hours," Emily's dad says.

Emily wants to say she knows this, because of what Jimmy inside her just said, but she doesn't. Nevertheless, she's sad that she cannot let her parents know what a wonderful son they have. To know this, yet be unable to see and talk to him, would, for them, be awful.

"Just now, we're all here to help Ava," Jimmy reminds his sister. "Not dwell in the past. Ask Sarah how things are going in her school with preparations for the Charity Run. She's bound to cheer our parents up."

Chapter Twenty-five

Sarah must have read Jimmy's mind through Emily. Or is it because of Claribel? Whatever, just now, after the revelation that Jimmy is *truly* her brother, in this world, Emily merely accepts it as a matter of course when Sarah, clutching her little doll, comes over to her and sits on her lap, asking...

"Can me and Claribel tell everyone here what's happening in our school? Please!"

"Ahem!" Emily exclaims. "Everyone listen to Sarah. She has something to tell us."

"And Claribel," the little girl adds, shyly. She gets up off Emily's lap, goes over to the table, where she carefully places Claribel, turns around, takes in a deep breath, then...

"Yesterday, Claribel persuaded Dad to take time off from work and come and speak with Mrs McLean, our head teacher, about the Charity Run. He picked me up from Sam's school to take me to *my* school. Claribel and I were the only kids 'cos it was Friday afternoon, but Mrs McLean was there. She said what we're doing for Ava is that Lord thing."

Sarah looks at Sam who grins.

"Laudable," explains Sam.

"That too," says Sarah. "And Dad and Mrs McLean, they sort of talk and talk and talk and it gets very boring, so me and Claribel make plans. I can't remember if it was my idea or Claribel's, but this is what we decided. That we ask Emily's granny to come to our school on Monday. Dad's arranging for someone to bring her. Or maybe it'll be a taxi... I don't really know..."

Sarah looks anxiously at Emily's granny.

"A taxi will do, love," Granny says.

"Well, she... Emily's granny... *she's* going to teach the *whole* school how to make muffins."

The word 'whole' is emphasised by Sarah spreading her small arms as widely as possible.

"Wow!" exclaims Emily's dad. "So, my mother-in-law will become famous all over again, Sarah. Another Mary Berry, ay!"

"Who's she?" asks Sarah, looking puzzled.

"Just about the most famous chef in the world."

"Can she make muffins like Emily's granny's?"

"I really don't know. Never asked. But please continue, Sarah."

"Well... if all the children make muffins and bring them along to the Charity Run on Wednesday then..." Sarah goes silent, as though trying to work out what comes after the 'then'. Violet helps her:

"Then Emily's granny won't have to make a thousand muffins all by herself, will she? What a wonderful idea, Sarah," she says.

"Actually, I think it was *my* idea and not Claribel's," Sam's little sister announces after noticing Sam looking at her so proudly. "But Claribel definitely thought up the Little Roo Run."

"Would that be for oldies like me?" jokes Emily's

granny.

"Oh no! Old people come later. No, the Little Roo Run will be for dolls like Claribel. And teddies and things like that."

"Soft animals," explains Sam.

"For the infant school kids. Boys can bring an Action Man. Or a Godzilla." Sarah looks thoughtful. "Or even a toy car. The little ones can bring whatever they want to bring for the Run to be spon... sponny-thingyed."

"Sponsored," corrects Sam.

"That's what I said. And Joey the kangaroo can take the lead." Sarah looks pleadingly at Kami. "Is that all right, Kami? You can be with him if you like."

"Fine by me," agrees Kami. "He'll be up to anything as long as he doesn't get chucked out of a window again."

"So..." Sarah takes in a long, deep breath, "*My* school decided that *we* start with the *Little* Roo Run. That'll be the little ones toddling down from Whitestone Pond to here in the Vale of Health. Then the toddlers and the dolls and stuff can all have their muffins and..."

Sarah pauses.

"And orange juice," adds Sam.

"Sam!"

"Sorry!"

"Muffins *and* orange juice while older kids like me and Sam and grownups too can run round the Heath up to the top of Parliament Hill. *After* that, old people like Emily's granny can just run down the hill to the

Highgate ponds. Or walk. With their walking frames. Easy-peasy!"

"So... it'll be like a relay, then?" suggests Kami.

Sarah looks thoughtful. She picks Claribel up from the table and studies the doll as if hoping she might get an answer.

"I've got it! They can each pass on a muffin. Instead of a bat-thing."

"Baton," corrects Sam.

"That's what I said," insists Sarah, frowning.

"So, we oldies will be eating all the muffins that are left over!" observes Emily's granny. She gleefully rubs her hands together.

"Not exactly *all*," says Sarah, looking worried.

Emily's father starts to clap, her mother joins in, and soon, that little house in the Vale of Health is filled with applause whilst Ava and Lingling are still lost, together, in the glorious music of Franz Schubert flowing out from the music room across the landing.

Sarah takes a little bow, picks up Claribel and helps the doll to bow as well before grabbing a couple of muffins off a plate on the table, one for herself and the other for Claribel who requires assistance to devour *her* muffin.

*****

The music stops. Moments later, Lingling appears with Ava. More clapping from hands still sore after clapping for Sarah and Claribel before the two young pianists attack the muffins.

"That was brilliant, Ava. You're so good you could

easily take my place at the festival next month," suggests Emily.

"No. I've heard you two play together in the music room at school. Better than anything I've heard on *You Tube*. Surely your hand will be better then?"

"Worth a try!" asserts Emily before her granny beckons her.

"You and me. The music room," she whispers. There's a seriousness in the old lady's expression that unnerves the granddaughter. Together, unnoticed by others, they slip out of the sitting room into a room so recently filled by Schubert in the form of his ethereal Fantasy duet that the great composer's presence still hangs in the silent air. Emily closes the door behind her.

"She's good, but you are so much better. Have you been doing those finger exercises I suggested?" asks the girl's granny.

Soon, grandmother and granddaughter are sitting side by side on the piano stool facing away from the instrument.

"Trying to, but my fingers still feel like overcooked sausages," the girl replies. "Kind of stiff and rubbery."

Granny chuckles.

"And it *really* was an accident? I find this so hard to believe. I've always told you to be so very careful with your hands and fingers. Must be worth a fortune with that talent of yours."

"Like I said, Granny. My hand got trapped and the locker door swung shut on it."

"That is not what Jimmy saw according to Jenny."

"You two still...?"

"Oh, yes! We do," interrupted Granny. "But I do understand why you want to blame yourself. Particularly since you've only just got some of your friends back." She pauses. "Half-Italian, I hear. Belinda."

"And looks like a bloody Hollywood film star!"

"Just be careful, Emily. Perhaps you're right. Forgive and forget, ay? Anyway, that's not why I really brought you into the music room alone." She pats the keyboard lid of the piano. "This Steinway behind us is now yours. As is my house. Deeds transferred into your name today. Your dad has them safe."

Emily doesn't know whether to feel happy or worried.

"Why?" she asks.

"Let's just say, Jenny's coming with me. We thought Jimmy should know, too."

"Can't *she* tell him you're going away. Will this be another concert tour, Granny? At your age?"

"Bit more than that. No, I worried that if *she* tells Jimmy, he might get the wrong idea. She really is too old for him, anyway. Better coming from you. And he still has one last job to do. For him, the most important. Jenny's listening to right me now and she agrees."

But Jimmy is listening as well, and when Emily and her granny look at each other he enters the old lady, alone...

Chapter Twenty-six

There's a very distinctive smell before Jimmy finds himself in a hospital again...

Emily's granny was seated in a waiting room until her name got called out. She stood up and followed a nurse into the consulting room where the consultant, a woman much the same age as her daughter, sat behind a desk poring over a case file. The woman looked up, smiled, introduced herself and asked the old lady to sit down. All present, including Jimmy, knew what was coming, but it had to be said. Spelt out, even, but without using the 'D-word'.

"That discomfort in your chest and the feeling of food sticking when you swallow..." the doctor began. "We have an explanation from your scan here." She turned the computer screen around. All black and white, like the keyboard of the old lady's piano. Made no sense to Emily's granny until, bit by bit, the doctor brought it to life. And impending death.

"This aortic arch aneurysm you've just shown me?" Granny asked. "Can anything be done?"

"I've referred you to the vascular surgeon because of the size of the aneurysm. Only *he* can answer that question for you."

"An operation, then?"

The doctor nodded her head, slowly... thoughtfully.

"Really big. And quite risky," she explained.

"What if nothing's done? I mean the pain's not that

bad, and I can cope with the food sticking as long as I wash it down with something."

"It'll get even bigger with time, and the main risk is rupture. The aneurysm could burst at any time."

"And from what you say, the operation might produce the same result." Granny had no fear of using the D-word. "Either way, I could die."

"True," replied the doctor, nodding again.

She reminds me of that light-sensitive nodding figure I saw with Emily in one of her friend's homes, thinks Jimmy.

"Thank you, doctor, for being blunt. I'll see what that surgeon fellow has to say, then. Talk it over with my family. And with my granddaughter."

"Your granddaughter? How old is she?"

"Fifteen. And a better Schubert pianist than I ever was."

The doctor looks down at her patient's case file.

"Yes... I can see you were a pianist."

Emily's granny grins, holds up her hands and waggles her knobbly fingers at the doctor.

"Still am. And will be until that aneurysm has some other plan for me. So, I'll just wait to hear from that vascular surgeon, right?"

"Indeed. I hope he can do something. And keep you playing that piano for a good while longer."

The old lady gets up and leaves before Jimmy returns from his grandmother's hidden place of memories to the real world outside.

*****

"I know," Emily says, a tear truckling down her cheek. "About the aneurysm."

"Jimmy, ay?"

Emily nods and wipes away the tear.

"He does get around, that brother of yours! And all because of Jenny. I hope he won't miss her *too* much. They've become really good mates. She told me that if she was sixty years younger, she might think about it, but I believe she knows your brother has his own future. He's been thinking things out, recently, she tells me. To do with science which really isn't her thing."

Emily chuckles.

"Nor mine! And he goes on and on about my friends, he does. Lingling's little Chinese nose, Kami's blue eyes, Sam's figure, Violet's hair. Does my head in. I keep telling him to shut up!"

"It'll work out, Emily. Things always do. Meanwhile, you, me and your piano? How about us playing the Debussy that should have won you first prize in the North London Festival last year, huh? *En Bateau*. We'll row that boat together, ay? Do you need the score, or is it still inside your head? With Jimmy?"

"Jimmy's really not into classical music, you know. Rap's his thing. Can't think why. It's all just jabber, jabber, jabber to me."

"The Debussy score?"

"No need. Still in my head. I'll play secondo, left hand only."

"Better than nothing. And you can say hello to your new one-hundred-and-twenty-two-year-old Steinway piano. You know, I'm really glad to know there's something in this room older than me."

Emily laughs. Jimmy, too. And he leaves. Like Schubert, Debussy's not his thing.

What and who is our granny talking about when she says Jenny knows I have my own future? he's thinking.

One last job to do? But will Emily agree?

Chapter Twenty-seven

Early Monday morning, after rubbing away the sleep from her eyes, Emily checks her mobile beside her bed for messages...

Dozens!

"Oh my God!" she whispers to herself.

"You'll not get any help from him," mutters Jimmy. "I should know. What's the problem."

Without answering, Emily trawls through cruel untraceable comments on Snapchat, Instagram and Facebook, concerning Ava and the Roo Run.

'Run for the Russians? No way!'

'It's a scam, guys. He's gonna use the money to do up his yacht in Benidorm.'

'Say 'No!' to the Roo Run. Keep you money safe!'

Most sickening of all is a recording of the beautiful Belinda saying the Roo Run money will be used by the Russians to make missiles to drop on Ukraine and that Ava's dad is, *'Hiding in their loft'.*

It just went on and on. Emily put down her phone.

"Call Ava," suggests Jimmy. "It's got to be Belinda who started this."

Emily does as instructed. Ava, still in bed when she answers the phone, can hardly speak through her tears.

"Why?" she asks Emily. "We were such good friends. I told her you were only trying to help me. But she just went on and on and on about letting her down, that she had it all sorted, and now..."

"That bit in the recording about your dad hiding in the loft all along, pretending he's been kidnapped, it's horrid. Ugh! I could kill that girl."

"But she's not like that, Em. I just don't understand. Something's going on. Must be."

"See you outside school, Ava. I'll get there early. We'll go together to see Mrs Gray. She's got to put a stop to this or there *will* be no Roo Run."

Jimmy keeps on at Emily to give him access to Belinda's hippocampus, find out why, and she keeps on at him to shut up and let her concentrate. When they do meet up with Ava and Mrs Gray, in the head teacher's office, before assembly, they learn that the woman is as deeply shocked as they are.

"Don't worry, Ava. I'll say something at assembly. We won't let those hooligans derail the Roo Run." But no mention of Belinda.

There's a knock on the door. The school secretary appears.

"It's the police," she says. "They want a word with you. In private."

The girls pass a scruffily dressed guy on their way out through the secretary's office.

"A policeman?" queries Ava.

"Plain clothes," responds Emily. "Remind me never to date a policeman!"

"But why?"

Prior to assembly, things go from bad to worse. Ava gets called names. "Go back to Russia!" one girl whispers, brushing past her. "Poo Run, not Roo Run!"

another says. Only Kami, Sam, Violet and Lingling seem to remain on board for the big event on Wednesday. Belinda, meanwhile, struts about like a celebrity model at a fashion parade, with girls flocking all around her. When Ava tries to talk to her, and find out why, the half-Italian girl looks the other way.

At assembly, Mrs Gray tells the school to ignore rumours spreading through social media sites 'like escaping sewage' ("Wow, she's furious," comments Jimmy), and that the Roo Run is most definitely going ahead. She also tells the school that the police are taking the matter very seriously indeed.

"Poor woman," whispers Jimmy. "She looks shattered and it's only Monday morning."

Mrs Gray's assurances do little to assuage concern amongst a number of girls at the school that the Roo Run is a scam and that Ava's dad is 'out to get everyone's money'. Belinda, who denies initiating the rumours, enjoys a whistleblower's glory by heading the 'Anti-Roo Run campaign'. She organises protest meetings during breaks, and, one by one, Roo Run supporters desert the fold and join her. By Tuesday afternoon, it seems that Emily and her five re-found friends will be the only girls from her school who will be running on Wednesday.

"Thank heavens for Sarah and *her* school," says Jimmy as Emily makes her way home that afternoon. "And maybe Granny can rustle up a few oldies with or without walking sticks and Zimmer frames."

"Sarah told Sam that they'll be making enough

muffins at her school tomorrow morning to feed the five thousand, like in the bible. Hmm! Five, more like," Emily tells her brother.

"Don't give up, sis. Plus, you have your friends back, at least."

"I'm not worried about me. It's Ava, poor girl. Her dad's disappeared, for God's sake. All their money gone. He'd never do that to her. Of course it's not a scam."

"And Belinda's not scum. Not to look at, anyway. What the hell's happening, Emily?"

Emily's parents try to persuade their daughter to ignore the vicious social media 'hate wave'.

"Good one, Emily" whispers Jimmy. "It's so like a 'heat wave'. Nothing you guys can do about it other than sit it out."

But what is revealed to the family as they sit watching a sit-com on the television, evening meal on trays on laps, stops that wave in its slippery tracks...

Breaking News...

The body of the missing Russian scientist, Nikolai Ivanov, was discovered by police frogmen trawling the River Thames today on information received. Police are treating his death as suspicious, suicide having been ruled out.

Mr Ivanov, a staunch critic of Putin's invasion of Ukraine, had received death threats following his support of the deceased rival to the Russian President, Alexei Navalny, thought to have been murdered in prison on Putin's command.

Mr Ivanov's daughter, Ava, together with her schoolfriends, and those of the sister of one of these friends, has organised a charity run, named the Roo Run after a soft animal belonging to one of those girls, which is to take place tomorrow afternoon on Hampstead Heath, starting at Whitestone Pond at 2 p.m. The proceeds will help provide for the deceased man's wife and daughter who have been left penniless by the scientist's killers.

"Oh my God!" exclaims Emily. "Poor, poor Ava. I can't believe it. We have to help her. Do you think this newsflash will make a difference? Like a few more than five of us running tomorrow?"

Emily's mum puts her food tray aside and comes over to hug her daughter.

"It *will* make a difference. You'll see."

Chapter Twenty-eight.

With media coverage, the turnout on Hampstead Heath, Wednesday afternoon, is massive. Large numbers of police are involved, and Emily has to swallow her words about not dating policemen when she sees some of the younger male officers.

'*If only*' she thinks, blushing, when one particularly handsome young officer looks at, and smiles at her, all ready for the run in her tracksuit.

"Seems Sarah's pals are gonna need a lot more than five thousand muffins for this lot," Jimmy says to Emily, snapping her out of a schoolgirl reverie.

"They have help. Look over there. A hot dog stand. And an ice cream van on the other side of the pond. Plus, there are still crowds coming from all directions. This is gonna be..."

Emily pauses.

"Huge?" suggests Jimmy.

"More than!" his sister replies. "Hey! There's Ava and her mum. Getting out of that police car!"

A police car has just pulled up on the other side of Whitestone Pond, and Ava, followed by her mother, emerges from the back. A young, female, uniformed officer accompanies them to join Emily. The two friends, both weepy, hug, and, not long afterwards, they're joined by Violet and Kami who arrive together. Finally, a 210 bus is allowed through the police cordon, and out of it pours a throng of infants together with Sam, Sarah and, of course, Joey the soft toy kangaroo.

It is *his* event, after all!

Naturally, Sarah takes over the organisation of the 'Little Roo Run' with some assistance from the children's parents and teachers. As this isn't a race but merely a sponsored charity run, there's no actual beginning, no starting pistol or cheering. The little children just start toddling off down the hill towards the Vale of Health where promises of muffins will, hopefully, be fulfilled. A vanload was collected from Sarah's school just before lunch. Not exactly created by Junior Bake-off winners, but, after Emily's granny's lesson on muffin making for the whole school on Monday morning, surely destined to please young tummies. And *these* muffins are complimented by lorry loads from professional bakeries.

The children keep coming and coming as Emily, her friends, little Sarah and Joey head off down the hill to start their section of the run, each clutching a sponsorship sheet with a list of names and corresponding amounts of money for the fund to help Ava and her mother, both of whom will be also be running.

Jimmy, too, enjoys the run, although wishes he could swop places with his sister, give her a rest and puff and pant on her behalf whilst she cools out inside his head. Something that his overactive brain keeps trying to figure out whenever he can persuade Emily to visit one of the many science websites he's been hooked on since ogling her gorgeous schoolfriends through her own eyes.

'*What am I doing inside here?*' he keeps asking himself. '*Will I ever get out? Jenny insists she's too old, otherwise she and I could make something of it together in that alternative reality. Maybe I should have left before? But I knew I had to hang around for Emily. She needs me, although now...*'

Despite what happened to Ava's father, a truly brave soul, Emily now looks happy. '*Friends do that for you,*' Jimmy reckons as he bounces up and down inside his sister's head to the rhythm of her running.

Emily stops, stooping down to take a breather, and, briefly, Jimmy sees the world out there upside down.

'*Reality flipped? The sky becomes the ground, gravity reversed? If only Ava's dad, the scientist, was still alive, I could've asked him how to reverse things back for myself. I somehow always knew that it all began for me out there in what they call the real world.*'

Whilst inside his sister's brain for the rest of the Roo Run, Jimmy uses his own tired-though-active brain to go over what he's learned about the nature of reality. Slowly, patterns, shapes and mathematical equations take shape, and begin make sense, guided by one word he's heard so often, but never properly understood, through his sister's ears...

Love.

*****

Shattered and muffed-out, the five friends end up on the floor at Emily's granny's in the Vale of Health. Like post-Olympic athletes, which, being classical musicians

179

they most definitely are *not*, they flex and stretch their arms and legs before lying back and staring up at the ceiling.

"Give us a song, Violet," says Lingling. "I'm much too tired to play the piano."

"Just now, I think I'd sound a bit like a strangled frog if I tried to sing," replies Violet.

Ava gets up.

"I'll play. For my dad. The Moonlight Sonata. You'll all know what Paul Lewis said about the first movement on the television. It's so very true. I've been playing it in my head ever since the police came round to tell me and Mum they found his body in the Thames."

Whilst Ava and Beethoven come to terms with death in that legendary piece of music that has never had anything to do with the moon—like the Schubert piece, it's a 'fantasy', Ava insists—Emily's dad enters the room.

"At the latest estimate, you girls have raised over £50,000 for Ava and her mum. Putin's brutes haven't destroyed everything that Ava's dad stood for."

"Joey helped," insists little Sarah now standing behind Emily's parents, Joey the kangaroo dangling from one hand, Claribel from the other. "But I think he wants to get back to Kami now," she continues, returning the cuddly marsupial to its owner. "I wish I had one. As well as Claribel," she adds. "Can you only get them in Australia? Kangaroos, I mean. Not Claribels."

Kami laughs. Jimmy loves to hear her girlish

laughter after so much sadness and pain. How relieved he feels to have helped rid the girl of her evil brother. Priest indeed! He wonders how her father is adjusting to the knowledge that his own son is an incestuous paedophile lucky to escape a jail sentence. And through Emily's eyes, he can see the Chinese girl, now so happy to have back her own father who, like Ava's, only wished good things for others, had been released from wrongful imprisonment by the Chinese, because of his and Emily's granny. He glimpses Sam, feeling almost ashamed to admire her lovely legs; Sam whose pointless sisterly jealousy had given way to love for her delightful little sister because of *his* sister. And finally, he focuses on the dark-haired Violet whose parents saw sense after a Roo Club meeting that persuaded them to think of their only daughter and not only themselves.

'Time to move on?' he wonders. *'But where? How? And with whom?'*

*****

The following morning, during break, Emily and Ava are called into the head teacher's office. Ava's mother is there, and, as they enter the room, she gets up, gives her daughter a hug, then hugs Emily.

"Mrs Ivanov wants to thank you personally," says Mrs Gray. "But she and Ava have something else to say, she tells me. Please, each of you girls... draw up a chair."

After sitting down, Emily learns that the final amount made the previous day is over £115,000.

"I believe you, Emily, are the one I must thank the most," Mrs Ivanov begins, "but there's something else needs to be said." She looks pointedly at her daughter.

"I'm so sorry, Emily," says Ava, looking down at her hands. "For being mean to you before... you know."

Emily looks at her, not knowing what to say.

"Tell her it wasn't her fault," whispers Jimmy. "It's all about Belinda. Ava got sucked into her circle."

"It wasn't your fault," says Emily.

"Belinda!" whispers Jimmy. "Say it!"

"I can't," says Emily aloud.

Ava turns to look at Emily, clearly puzzled.

"Can't what, Emily?"

"Can't play with Lingling at the North London Festival of Music and Drama competition. Only two weeks away now. Not with this hand of mine." She lifts up her injured hand. "Will you take my place, Ava?"

"I... I don't know, Emily. It's a difficult piece. I could..."

"I don't want to let Lingling down. Not after what she's been through with her own dad having been in prison on China."

"Of course she will," interrupts Mrs Ivanov.

There's a knock on the door. It opens and the school secretary's face appears.

"Belinda Contini wants to see you, Mrs Gray," the woman says.

"Talk of the devil," Jimmy whispers to his sister.

"Show her in," says Mrs Gray. "The more the merrier."

Belinda, looking as lovely as ever, enters. The door closes behind her. Neither Emily nor Ava want to look at her. Jimmy does but doesn't dare tell his sister.

'If only I didn't have to rely on Emily's eyes all the time,' he says to himself.

"Please, Mrs Gray, believe me that video recording about the Roo Run had nothing to do with me," she says, trying to catch Ava's attention, but the other girl keeps her head down. "I'd never do anything like that. I told Ava my dad and uncle want to help as well. Now Uncle's promised to match what you've made pound for pound."

"That's really kind of him, Belinda," says Ava's mum. "But truly, it's far too generous. Thank you, all the same."

Belinda looks at Mrs Gray. Neither Emily nor Jimmy can make out her expression. Is she smiling or not?

"I've never dared say 'No' to my dad," the half-Italian girl says.

"Tell your father I'll give him a call," the head teacher says, "and as for that other business, it's all water under the bridge. The Roo Run was an enormous success thanks to Emily and her friends in the Roo Club."

"It's a really good thing they're doing," Belinda says. Neither Emily nor Ava looks at her, but Emily does respond with a quiet,

"Thank you!"

'God, she's lovely,' thinks Jimmy savouring a quick glance from Emily as the half-Italian girl gets up to leave the room. *"But why are you protecting her?"* he

asks his sister inside her head. *"It had to be her who started the rumours about Ava's dad hiding in their loft all the time. And as for that cruel online video recording!"*

Emily shrugs her shoulders. Mrs Gray laughs. Belinda looks anxiously sideways at Emily.

"Why did you just shrug your shoulders, Emily?" the head teacher asks.

"I don't really know," the girl answers, truthfully. The truth is, she honestly does *not* know why she should protect the girl when, because of *her*, fearful and friendless, things got so bad that she wanted to take her own life.

"Emily, would you stay behind, please," the head teacher says.

Apart from Jimmy, who can hardly wait to know what it is Mrs Gray has to say to his sister in private, the others leave, with Mrs Ivanov again verbalising her sincere gratitude to Emily for all that she's doing for her and Ava.

"Your grandmother," the head teacher begins. "Such a wonderful woman. And a world class musician. We were thinking..." She pauses as if wondering how to express what she means to say.

"Yes?" questions Emily, puzzled. What comes next, however, is a pleasant surprise.

"You know, it really has been such an honour to have the granddaughter of the one of the greatest Beethoven pianists of all time in our school. And she told me, once, that one day you will even surpass her."

"I'm more of a Schubert person, really," says Emily, grinning tearfully.

"Beethoven will come to you. When you're a little older. That's for sure. No, what I really want to ask you... and please do say if you're not happy with my suggestion... what I wondered was whether you would think about some of you musical girls here giving a public concert in your grandmother's honour some time. And when your hand's fully recovered. Next term? A memorial concert for Ava's dad too, perhaps?"

Emily is so happy that she cannot hold back. She gets up, goes around to the other side of the head teacher's desk, puts her arms around the woman and gives her a big hug.

"Granny will love that, I just know she will. And we can practise in her home which now belongs to me. Her Steinway, too."

"She told me," Mrs Gray said. "Told me about Jimmy, too. And how her imaginary own friend, Jenny, helped *her* as a child."

Chapter Twenty-nine

On her way home from school, that afternoon, Emily has never felt happier. They had a great time over lunch break, all six of them, sharing thoughts and views about various boys who had eagerly joined the charity run, with Emily waxing lyrical about that handsome young police officer. He was still in her head, displacing Jimmy, when she opened the front door, only to be met, immediately, by her tearful mother who threw her arms around her. Emily knew before any words were spoken.

"It's Granny, isn't it?" she asked.

Her mother nodded. Before saying anything, she took Emily into the kitchen. They sat together at the table and the girl's mum took hold of her hand.

"The hospital rang. Just before you came home."

"It burst, then? The aneurysm?"

"Uh-huh!"

"Is she...?" Emily couldn't say the word. It wouldn't come out. Jimmy didn't want to hear it either.

"There was nothing they could do, the nurse told me over the phone."

"She knew it was coming," Emily said. "And I don't think she'd have wanted to go through with a big operation. It would've been touch and go, anyway."

"So... her house, her piano, are all yours, now, Emily."

"She told me that, too. But I don't know anything about looking after houses. I can still stay here, with you and Dad, can't I?"

Emily's mother laughs through her tears and puts her arm around her daughter.

"Don't be silly! Of course you can. And Dad will sort out all the legal stuff till you're older."

Emily had to push away happier thoughts of herself and a certain handsome young police officer moving in together into the house in the Vale of Health, allowing Jimmy to say his piece inside her head.

"You and your friends could use it at weekends. For your music," he suggests.

"Could me and my friends go there at weekends? Chill out? Play music?"

"Parties and raves, eh?"

"No, Mum! That would be disrespectful to Granny. I'm serious. Perhaps Ava could give piano lessons to little kids to make some extra money."

"You'd let them loose on your precious Steinway?"

"Maybe not. But we could start up musical weekends. And Sarah can come and make muffins for us. Granny taught her whole school how to make them before the Roo Run."

"I know. Granny had a great time. Told me all about it. There was more flour on the children and on the floor than in the muffins, she said."

"I'll miss Granny so much. But for her I might've..." Emily pauses.

"No, you wouldn't have. She told me about that weekend. How lonely you felt because you'd lost all your friends at school."

"It was Granny who helped me most. And..." Emily pauses. Why she never wanted to talk to her parents about Jimmy, she remains unsure.

"And your imaginary brother, right?" the girl's mother says for her.

*****

"Do you remember?" Emily asks her brother whilst lying in bed later that evening. His response,

"Remember what?"

"What it's like. After you... you know... like Granny." Still, she cannot say the word. Jimmy helps her:

"Kicked the bucket as a neonate in that incubator? Nothing! Didn't know I *was* once your brother in this world till I entered our mum's hippocampus. Saw myself lying there, in a neonatal intensive care unit, not moving. Funnily, it wasn't me I was concerned about. I mean, I was gone anyway and probably hadn't a clue what it was all about. But for Mum and Dad... bloody awful! And that lovely head teacher of yours lost a child, too. Do you think it's kind of made them all stronger?"

"In what way?" asks Emily.

"Every way."

"Maybe. I guess Mr and Mrs Frobisher, Kami's parents, must feel the same about that son of theirs. What he did to Kami. Must be like he's dead to them after they found out."

"That head priest guy..."

"The Spiritual Director at the Seminary?"

"Him. Seemed a wise guy to me."

"You're right. *He's* the real saint. Not that bastard, Mark. She's still pretty traumatised, you know," Emily says. "And it was going on for years and years. Poor Kami!"

"Plus, but for Joey the kangaroo, things could have got even worse. Just think... what Belinda did to you is nothing compared with what that bugger got up to."

"The pervy priest of a brother bugger?"

"Never will be a priest now, thank God. You know, I was thinking about Belinda, back then."

"Back when?"

"At the seminary. Don't know why. Do you realise she's the only one of your classmates I've not seen out of school uniform?"

"Why would you want—?"

"What d'you think she'd look like in casual clothes?" interrupts Jimmy. "Or Sunday best. She has to be Catholic too, being Italian."

"She'd look just the same. Horrible!"

"Somehow, I can see her in white. Like in a wedding dress."

"Oh, do shut up about bloody Belinda!"

"Why do you think she came to see Mrs Gray? I mean, that video recording of hers. Could it really be an AI fake? Perhaps we've got it wrong about her."

"The only wrong thing about Belinda is that she was ever let into our school in the first place. Anyway, getting back to Granny. She'll be someplace else. Has to be. Can't suddenly not exist. So, you honestly cannot remember a thing between what you saw inside Mum's hippocampus and your earliest memories when you were inside me?"

"Not a thing!" affirms Jimmy.

"And Jenny. Do you still see her? Talk with her?"

"Gone too. Just like Granny."

Turning over onto her back, Emily stares at the ceiling, half-hoping she might see her granny's smiling, wrinkled face up there.

"It's Friday tomorrow. Another Roo Club meeting. D'you think we'll be overwhelmed if Mrs Gray makes an announcement at assembly? Other girls wanting us to crowd fund for them to go on skiing holidays? Or jet set to the Bahamas with their boyfriends?"

"Do you think Belinda's been to the Bahamas? 'Cos her uncle's rolling in money."

"Dunno and don't care!"

"So who could have started the anti-Roo Run campaign, then, if it wasn't Belinda?"

"Shut up about bloody Belinda! Go to sleep!"

Chapter Thirty

Saturday morning. Exhausted after a day full of sadness over Granny's death (she finally finds courage to say the D-word) and other girls' woes, both during the Roo Club meeting and at break time, plus a night full of troubled dreams, Emily's mobile phone pings. To her horror, it's a message from Belinda. Just when she's beginning to feel she can get her life back together again, and move on beyond her disappointment about the North London Festival of Music and Drama, the pain of all that bullying comes flooding back. Plus, of all places, her nemesis wants to meet her at the very pond on Parliament Hill Fields where, in the recent past, she seriously thought about ending it all...

Because of Belinda.

"Go!" urges Jimmy. "Maybe we'll finally get to the truth."

"There is only one truth!" insists his sister. "Belinda is a bully who, but for you, would have killed me. Perhaps she wants to do the job herself, now. Fill my pockets with stones, push me into the pond and walk away."

"I don't think so. This is a cry for help."

"Me help Belinda?"

"You helped all those others who bullied you. Turned their lives around."

"Belinda's different. She's..." Emily pauses as she searches for the right word to describe the girl who, during a dark period of her life that seemed to go on forever, turned every day into a nightmare. Jimmy finds the word for her. From inside her brain.

"Evil?" he suggests.

"Evil," she repeats.

"All the more reason to go. Now! Destroy that evil."

"What if she destroys me?"

"She won't. And I'm telling you, this is a cry for help."

"How do you know?"

"I just do."

*****

An hour later, Emily sees her arch enemy sitting alone on that bench beside the pond. As with the last time she was there, when so very close to ending her life because of that girl on the bench, the ducks were busily preening themselves at the water's edge. When she quietly approaches the bench, the ducks appear to sense her arrival. In a collective fuss of flapping wings and angry quacks, they retreat to the safety of middle of the pond. A place of certain death for troubled girls with pockets full of pebbles.

Belinda turns around to look over her shoulder on hearing Emily call her name from a safe distance. Even from twenty yards away, Jimmy can see, through his sister's eyes, that the evil they spoke of is not coming from the girl herself, but from what she's going through.

"It's okay. You can sit down beside her," he says to Emily. "She wants to drown herself. I can tell, even from this distance."

Emily does as she's told to do by her brother. Uneasily, and without uttering a word, she sits down beside the girl who stole her friends away not so very long ago.

"Tables are turned, brother," Emily says silently to Jimmy. "*She's* the friendless one now. Not so happy when she's getting a taste of her own medicine."

"*Not* the same!" Jimmy points out. "You were never once mean to her. That's not why she's here. Look at her, for Pete's sake. Let me into her eyes."

"So?" queries Emily. "Why?"

"Did you just come here to gloat?" Belinda asks, staring ahead, looking at the ducks...

...Or at nothing?

"No. Jimmy told me to."

"Your brother who doesn't exist?"

"He does. More so than you could ever dream of."

Belinda turns to look Emily properly in the eye for the very first time. Jimmy is so relieved that Jenny, who mysteriously reappeared after Emily received that phone call, has agreed to come with him, for what he sees, even before taking that leap across realities, fills him with dread. Before he has time to think about summoning the courage to leave Emily, Jenny pulls him by the arm into the other girl's eyes from where, via her optic nerves, they enter a place so chilling that they have to hold onto each other...

*****

Belinda is seated, alone, in her school uniform, in the back of a car. Jimmy can only see the backs of the heads of the two men in the front, although he occasionally gets glimpses of the eyes of the driver. 'Evil' would not be a strong enough word to describe what he sees in those eyes, and this is reflected in the fear he senses in the girl. Judging by the greying hair, and slight balding, he is middle-aged or older, and Jimmy senses that she knows the man.

"Not far from here, Belinda," the older guy said. "And make sure you behave like I told you to, eh?"

"That accent?" whispers Jenny.

"Italian, I think. Jesus, man, this is like a bloody horror movie!" says Jimmy.

"About to become a movie star, ay? Your dad will be so very proud of you!" the foreign man continued, as though he had overheard Jimmy whispering from inside Belinda's hippocampus.

The girl in the back seat remained silent, though clearly terrified. The vehicle made an abrupt turn, came to a halt, the driver pointed a controller at an automatic door ahead, causing it to rise up, opening like the jaws of a carnivorous prehistoric monster, and the car started up again, moving on into the eerie darkness before the automatic door slammed noisily shut behind them.

Silence. Lights flickered on to reveal what appeared to be a large, empty warehouse.

"What on earth is going on?" questions Jimmy.

"This is bad," responds Jenny. "Like *really* bad!"

"Out you get, my lovely young actress!" the older man commands.

The driver, younger, and with a grin that would chill a frozen chicken, looked round at Belinda.

"Do as your uncle says, Belinda Bellina," he smirks in a similar, Italian accent. "And please do not upset him. His boss over there can get very nasty when angry."

Standing a few yards away from the car, arms folded, is a man with a black beard and wearing dark glasses.

The Devil himself? wonders Jimmy.

"Don't get out of the car, don't get out," he tries to warn the girl, but she cannot hear him. He's stuck in her hippocampus, and he knows that what he witnesses in the present has already happened in the past. When, he has no idea.

Belinda emerged from the vehicle and, like an automaton, followed her uncle, the younger driver and the Devil guy. At the far end of the warehouse, they entered a room. It looked like a bedroom, only there was a movie camera on a tripod manned by a fourth man in rolled-up shirt sleeves. The door closed behind Belinda. Jimmy saw the girl's uncle grab her by the arm and pull her towards the bed. He ordered her to sit down and smile at the camera.

"Remember, Belinda, you're doing this for Daddykins. He owes me big time. Always has done. And seeing you , all grown up like, in your confirmation dress, gave me the idea. An offer your daddy can't refuse, as our Camorra friends back in Naples would say. So, smile like you *really* want it!"

Belinda, facing the camera, now recording, attempted a smile, but Jimmy sees only fear in those beautiful eyes. And as he watches the bearded man mime the removal of his own top, what the bastard wanted the girl to do is only to clear. Before witnessing what was about to happen after Belinda's hands reach up to undo her school tie, the image goes fuzzy, then cuts out as though the owner of the memory of what happened next has tried to erase it. Things come back into focus. A different scene. Belinda was standing in what seems to be an office, now wearing casual clothes and talking with a different grey-haired man who also spoke with an Italian accent.

"It'll be nothing, Belinda," he said. "Your Uncle Franco has been so good to me. To *us*. And he badly needs a girl actress of your age for the movie he's making. Says you could become famous overnight, huh?"

"Do I have a choice?" asked his daughter.

The man sighed, studied his laptop screen then shook his head slowly.

"Basta! Vai ad aiutare la tua madre!" he said with obvious irritation and without looking up at his daughter.

Blankness again, and a return of the awful fear Jimmy saw in the girl's eyes in that other recalled memory, only now it filled the air, almost suffocating him. They were back in that fake bedroom. This time, the bearded guy was sitting on the bed, naked. Belinda was standing, half-dressed, putting her school uniform back on, fumbling with the buttons on her blouse, crying her eyes out, being watched all the time by the man called Uncle Franco.

"Let's get outa here!" urges Jimmy. "Quick!" Jenny, also in shock, agrees.

Back inside the safety of his sister's brain, where time as he knows it is unchanged since first entering Belinda's hippocampus, Jimmy tells Emily the worst: that her tormentor has, herself, been tormented; forced to take part in the making of a movie that at best could be described as 'porn'... at worst, maybe something far more terrible. Like Emily, Belinda is only fifteen.

"I know," Emily says to Belinda.

"Know what?" Belinda asks, looking fearfully at the other girl.

"About your Uncle Franco. Your dad. And what they made you do. Did that man...?"

Jimmy knows his sister cannot come out with a word that seems even worse the 'death'. The word he and Jenny feared happened in that artificial bedroom in a warehouse probably somewhere on the outskirts of North London.

When the other girl nods, Jimmy feels sickened. Sure, she's beautiful, he reflects, having only really hated her before, but her God-given looks, he reckons, are not there to be used and abused by heaven knows how many paedos out there in the foul ether of cyberspace.

Emily shares Jimmy's thoughts.

"Come home with me," she says to Belinda. "You'll

be safe there. Remember? Both my parents are doctors. They'll help you."

Looking blankly at the ducks in the pond, Belinda nods.

"When did it happen?" Emily asks.

Belinda continues to stare at the ducks. She doesn't reply to the question. Then...

"Some guy came up to me at church after mass last Sunday. He–" the girl begins, but stops short, clearly unable to continue. Emily puts her arm around her.

"Sis... together, we'll get those guys put in jail. Tell her that," urges Jimmy.

"Belinda, my parents will be going to the police ASAP." Emily took out her mobile phone and sent an urgent, explicit message to her mother. "You cannot go back home. We're pretty much the same size. You can use my clothes."

"My little sister," whispers Belinda. "I'm worried they'll do something to *her* now. She's only ten."

"Your sister too," says Emily before sending her mother another message.

Jimmy has a thought...

"Ask Belinda whether her mum knew any of this."

Emily does. Belinda shakes her head. Her reply is chilling.

"Uncle Franco said, afterwards, 'Tell your mum and she's dead meat.'"

Emily makes yet another call to her mother...

'*B's mum too*'

"When did it happen?" asks Emily.

Belinda is staring vacantly at the ducks in the pond.

"I can't swim," is her answer.

"Tell me," insists Emily. "Was it recently?"

"Last month. Then..." She turns to look at Emily again. Jimmy chances it alone, leaving Jenny inside Emily.

Almost immediately, Belinda, her little sister and their parents were leaving church after mass. Belinda, looking gorgeous in her Sunday best, was trailing behind the others. An old guy grabbed her arm from behind just as her family turned a corner ahead. A man who always sat in a pew by himself at the back of the church and stank of old socks. Belinda tried to pull herself free, but his grip was firm.

"I've seen the movie, Belinda," he growled with a sickening, toothless leer. "How about doing it with me some time, huh? Or would you rather I tell the entire world?"

His foetid breath clearly made Belinda want to vomit. She looked as though she about to scream when a woman's voice from behind called out,

"Are you all right, Belinda?"

The man let go and shuffled off. Belinda turned.

"Ignore Old Billy," said the woman. "He's been that way ever since his wife died... like a hundred years ago!" She paused, then frowned. "Are you okay?"

Belinda nodded, then hurried on around the corner to join her family how Jimmy, alone again, hurries back, away from the half-Italian girl's hippocampus, to Emily. He tells his sister and Jenny what he saw. Emily turns to Belinda, now staring again at the ducks...

"Last Sunday after mass, right? That smelly old fart? Jimmy told me."

"It's why I came here to end it all. In the pond. I just wanted to say sorry to you, first. I never–"

"I came here to do the same thing not long ago," interrupts Emily. "Drown myself. When I lost all my friends."

"Because of me."

"No, because of *me*. Not listening to others. Like my brother and granny."

Belinda is now in tears. It's the first time Emily has ever seen the girl cry. It makes Jimmy want to cry as well... if boys are allowed to.

"I can't begin to imagine what you've been through," Emily says, "but things will change from now on. Best friends forever?" The other girl nods and they touch elbows.

"'Billy' isn't it? The dirty old sod's name. He'll end his days in jail, too. My parents will see to that. Once my dad knows what's happened to you, he'll make damned sure all those bastards are locked up for good. Including your uncle. Plus, you and your sister and your mum will be totally safe with us. I promise."

"What about your brother, Jimmy?" asks Belinda. "When can I get to meet him?"

"Who knows? Maybe, one day?"

Chapter Thirty-one

Back home, whilst Emily's mum is showing Belinda's sister and mother their new, temporary accommodation in the spare room, and her father is explaining the situation to the police, over the phone, Belinda and Emily, together with Jimmy, sit watching the recording of the half-Italian girl going on about Ava's dad being hidden in the loft when, in truth, he was floating, face-down, in the River Thames.

"You must've all hated me so when you first saw this," Belinda says. "But that isn't me! I swear it."

Jimmy so wants to believe her, for that recording puts a dampener on the feelings he has for the girl. He's reminded of a book his sister had to read for English at school: 'The Strange Case of Dr Jekyll and Mr Hyde'. Could there be two Belindas? Will the bad one rear her not-so-ugly head again and do bad things to his little sister? Had they let a monster into their home?

Jimmy remembers Kami's mother's initial claim about the i-Phone recording made with the help of Joey the kangaroo and that nailed the perverted seminarian. AI?

"Emily, we might have the answer."

"Jimmy thinks we might have the answer," Emily says to Belinda. The other girl looks at her. Jimmy, his insides a turmoil when he looks at her eyes through his sister's, knows straightaway that there is no Miss Hyde lurking behind them.

"Sam's and Sarah's dad," he says.

"What about him?" asks Emily, in silence.

"Into IT. He could tell Joey's recording was no fake. What if this one *is* a fake? He's our man. He'll be able to tell."

Emily explains Jimmy's suggestion to Belinda. The tearful girl shrugs her shoulders.

"But it really looks like me. How can Sam's dad tell? And I never denied it back then because..." Belinda pauses.

"Because of what you'd been through. Jimmy and I understand. Look, I'm messaging Sam."

She does. Sam's reply is instantaneous.

'Dad and I coming to yours right now.'

Later, after Belinda is forced to verbally relive those awful moments in that fake bedroom for the police, and whilst a series of arrests are being made, Mr Frobisher sits with Emily and Belinda watching that horrid online recording over and over again, whilst Sam entertains Belinda's little sister.

"Belinda, do you have any selfies of yourself taken around the same time?" he asks.

"Of course," she replies. She taps her mobile to bring up all her recent photos and hands this to Sam's dad. He pauses and ponders over one particular image taken on the same day as the alleged recording. He enlarges it before handing the phone back to Belinda.

"Here's your proof."

"What?" whispers Jimmy.

"What?" echo Emily and Belinda together.

"That little spot on your chin. It's not there on the

video recording. Taken the same day judging by the date. Proof it's a fake recording. Can you think who might've done this?"

Belinda nods. Not wanting to tell Sam's dad about the other, genuine, video recording, she merely says,

"Uncle Franco. And he's going to jail, thanks to Emily and her dad."

Epilogue

Belinda's uncle, her father and all their accomplices, plus the smelly old widower from Belinda's church, are remanded in jail, awaiting trial. New and secret temporary premises, not far from Emily's place, are quickly found by Social Services for Belinda, her mother and her younger sister; temporary until, through the sale of the plush North London residence which was funded by the father's Camorra connections, a modest new home can be found.

Jimmy has vanished. Emily isn't too bothered, for now she and her re-found friends are all far too busy to be bothered with siblings. Particularly with that concert coming up as a double memorial in honour of both Ava's father and Emily's grandmother. Emily's brother having 'come of age', so to speak, can now move on in his life, Emily reckons. In that other reality. After all, he is two years her senior. However, when alone, she often recalls their last discussion with a certain nostalgia. It was a curious mix of Schubert and physics.

Physics had become Jimmy's chief passion. She would find herself spending (pointless) hours in front of her laptop screen visiting website after boring website dealing with the behaviour of ultra particles, mathematical equations that explain why the universe doesn't just rip itself apart, and, most of all, the ultimate mystery of reality.

And Schubert? Perhaps unwisely, before she

realised that she would be unable to play the Schubert F minor Fantasy with Lingling because of her hand injury, she explained to her brother, who still had little interest in classical music, why the music was so poignantly powerful.

"It's all about unrequited love," Emily explained to Jimmy one evening lying on her bed and staring up at the ceiling. "Like Schubert's *Wanderer Fantasy* and his *Winterreise* Song Cycle. There was this piano pupil of his, you see. Caroline Esterhazy. A Hungarian noblewoman. He'd known her, as a piano pupil, for several years, but as she grew into young womanhood, he fell deeply in love with her. We'll never know whether she felt the same way about him because of the way things were back then. She was an aristo. He wasn't. Case closed. He hadn't a chance and it broke his heart. But when she teasingly asked him why he had never dedicated any of his music to her, he stopped writing his Unfinished Symphony to compose the Fantasy which he did dedicate to Caroline. Then he went and died a year later. Only thirty-one. And it's all there. In the Fantasy in F minor."

"Which you never got to play because of Belinda."

"Allowing Lingling to shine when she so brazenly went to the piano, at the Festival Competition, on her own, and thumped out the Chopin Revolutionary Etude in a way that completely blew them away. All the anger she felt about what the Chinese Communist government had done to her family came out. No way could she win the duet section of the Competition, but they were all so amazed by her performance that she's already had a recording done and is in line for the next Young Musician of the Year title. Belinda did us all a favour."

"I do like Lingling's little Chinese nose," Jimmy said, having lost interest in Chopin and Schubert. "And Kami does have lovely blue eyes. Sam's figure is out of this world and Violet has amazing hair, Ava's legs are really cool, but... Love? For me? Where? How? And all that classical music would drive me mad. Prefer rap any day. Help me, sis!"

Poor Emily had no idea how to help her big brother trapped inside her head, but that was the very last time they spoke together.

*****

Monday morning. Belinda runs to catch up with Emily walking alone up the school driveway. She taps her new 'friend forever' on the shoulder.

"Hi!" Belinda greets.

Emily slows down.

"Hi there," she says. "How was your weekend?"

"You'll never guess!"

"I can try. You went shopping. Bought that top you were going on about on Friday."

"Love!"

"You gone daft, or something?"

"True!" insists Belinda. "At church, of all things. This gorgeous young guy's sitting at the back during mass, and afterwards he's kind of hanging around outside the church. He bows politely to mum... weird, I know... then looks at me and..."

Belinda blushes crimson.

"And?"

"I kind of melted. And he knows my name. Without me even telling him. We hang back behind my mum and sister and get to talking like we've always known each other. I can't believe how cool he is. Says he prefers rap when I said all my friends at school except for me are into classical music big time. And guess what?! He lives just around the corner from me. On his own. And we've got a date already. Tonight. Plus, I'll be sixteen next month."

"What's his name?" asks Emily out of curiosity.

"Jimmy, of all things. Bit boring. Would've preferred a Logan or a Duke or a Zach... but names aren't everything, are they?"

No, thinks Emily. *Names are not everything.*

The Author

Oliver Eade, born a Londoner and now an adopted Scot, retired from a career in hospital medicine thinking 'feet up and watch the TV', but this wasn't to be. After waking up one night with a ghost story in his head, he took to writing adult short stories. Over fifty have been published, several winning prizes, and some appear in two collections, **Walls of Words** and **Light & Dark Short Stories**.

His first young readers' book, **Moon Rabbit**, a magical journey to Mythological China (Oliver's wife is Chinese), was published in 2009. It was a winner of the *Writers' and Artists' 2007 New Novel Competition* and longlisted for the *Waterstones Children's Book Prize, 2008*. The sequel, **Monkey King's Revenge**, came out in 2011 and was a children's genre finalist for the *2012 People's Book Prize*. **Northwards**, a young readers' dark eco-fantasy based in Texas and the Arctic, was published in 2010. **The Rainbow Animal**, a fun spoof on war, is also set in North America where Oliver's son and two eldest granddaughters live. His short stories for young readers has been published as **Stories for Children Ages 7 to 77.**

No More Bamboo! is an illustrated book for younger children about a little panda who, fed up with eating nothing but bamboo, sets off alone (he thinks) in the forests of Western China to find more interesting food, only to encounter danger and discover that bamboo is the best nourishment for pandas, after all.

His debut adult novel, *A Single Petal*, which won the *Local Legend 2012 Spiritual Writing Competition*, is set in Tang Dynasty China. *Voices*, an adult novel of family love, intrigue, deceit and murder, is set in London whilst the *The Parth Path* is set in a post-apocalyptic Scotland run by women for women.

The Terminus, Oliver's debut young adult novel, returns to the city in which he was brought up; a city now changed beyond recognition from the drab post-World War II era and which, in a post-apocalyptic world, gives humankind a second chance. The *From Beast to God* trilogy, *The Golden Jaguar of the Sun*, *The Merging* and *Revelation*, follows a Texan boy and Mexican girl on a life-journey involving drug gangsters, ancient Aztec, Mayan and Native Mythology, blending European and Native American beliefs. The trilogy was revised, re-written and published as a three-part novel, *Eyes of Fire*, in 2023. *The Kelpie's Eyes* was inspired by a visit to the famous Scottish waterfall, the Grey Mare's Tail, and weaves Scottish mythology into a tale of sisterly love. It won the *2018 Georgina Hawtrey-Woore Young Adult Novel Award*.

Oliver has also written several plays, one of which, *The Gap*, inspired by being caught up in the Great Sichuan Earthquake of 2008, in China, and shortlisted for the *Rowan Tree One Act Play Competition*, went on tour in Scotland in 2012. Another, *The Other Cat*, a darkly humorous take on Schrödinger's famous feline, won the *2018 Segora International One Act Play Competition* and toured the Scottish Borders with two more of his plays in 2019. Twelve plays were published in 2024 as *The Other Cat & Other Plays*.

All the above books are available from Amazon.

Inspiration for *The Roo Club* came in a flash when the writer, whilst thinking about a fifteen-year-old-girl whom he and his wife know well, and whose school life had been made miserable by a clique of girl bullies, some of whom had once been the child's friends, saw an advert for a movie entitled 'Imaginary'; a horror movie, but the title made him wonder about children's 'so-called imaginary friends'. What, he suddenly wondered, if this girl he knew had an imaginary brother who could help her cope with the bullies? As for the connection with classical music, the author met his wife when, as teenagers, they played piano duets together, entering, as do Emily and Lingling in **The Roo Club**, the North London Festival of Music and Drama piano duet competition by playing Debussy's *En Bateau* and, like the fictional girls in the story, came second.

Although not confined to any particular genre, Oliver feels most comfortable in that magical space between reality and fantasy; the space into and out of which children slip so easily in their play; the place of dreams and myths and legends and deeply ingrained in many cultures across the globe.

Websites:
https://www.olivereadebooks.org/
https://oddproductionstheatre.weebly.com/

Contact: *olivereade'at'googlemail.com or via the first website above.*

Other Silver Quill Publishing books:

www.silverquillpublishing.com

Dream the Red Earth by Annette Reis, a debut novel for teens. Two girls, Keisha and Simi, experience loss in different ways.

The Stitched Record by Pamela Gordon Hoad, a historical novel about events just before and after the Norman conquest. Also ***Driftwood and Stone*** set in nineteenth century Sheffield and the **Harry Somers** series about a fifteenth century doctor-investigator.

Max's Diary-Tales of a time-travelling cat by Wendy Leighton-Porter to accompany the **Shadows of the Past** series bringing history to life, for children, through the adventures of brother and sister twins, their friend and the lovable and intelligent feline, Max.

The Atlantean Horse and other books for middle grade readers by the award-winning Cheryl Carpinello.

Autumn in August by Patricia Goodwin, for adults. Lucy carries a guilty secret. Will she maintain newfound independence or go with her heart?

The Pigeon Run by Robert Breustedt, for young adults. Four teenagers stumble across drug dealing close to home and get involved with something far more dangerous than they ever imagined.

Crying Through the Wind, and other adult books of the Oisin Kelly series, by Iona Carroll, which take the reader on a journey from rural 20th century Ireland to Australia, taking in the horror of a war in Vietnam. Also **Other Peoples' Lives**, a collection of adult short stories.

Susie in Spectra by Wendy Lake, a magical journey for middle grade readers over the Rainbow Highway to colourful lands of Spectra taken over by the evil Vileus. Can Susie and her new friend, Lemo, stop Vileus from plunging Spectra into eternal darkness?

No Relation by Christina Reis. An adult novel following the lives of two women, from different backgrounds, whose daughters later meet, unearthing disturbing and life-changing facts that devastate the two families.

The Adventures of Maxima and Coustaud, Books 1, 2 and 3, for children, by Sheikha Shamma, in which a magical horse and her funny bulldog companion must rescue a princess from a wicked witch... and more. Also, **The Colour Thief** about a young boy and his three pets who must save his city from losing all its colours to a mysterious colour thief, and **Who is Corona**, a colourfully illustrated e-book that has a simple message for young readers.

From Simon Leighton-Porter, **The Minerva System** in which IT developer Mansell's Minerva system attracts the wrong kind of attention 'in the City where no one cares if you scream', followed by **Death to Bankers**, '...simple, brutal and horribly real', adult thriller novels. Also **The Manhattan Deception**... 'Strike a deal with the devil or send one million people to their deaths?' and 'a cracking story from a talented writer', **Bomber Boys**... a journalist and former RAF officer, after devastating head injuries, is not only haunted by the past, but haunts the past himself in a struggle to return to the present day.